"The Object Lessons series achieves something very close to magic: the books take ordinary—even banal—objects and animate them with a rich history of invention, political struggle, science, and popular mythology. Filled with fascinating details and conveyed in sharp, accessible prose, the books make the everyday world come to life. Be warned: once you've read a few of these, you'll start walking around your house, picking up random objects, and musing aloud: 'I wonder what the story is behind this thing?'"

Steven Johnson, author of *Where Good Ideas Come From* and *How We Got to Now*

"Object Lessons describes themselves as 'short, beautiful books,' and to that, I'll say, amen. . . . If you read enough Object Lessons books, you'll fill your head with plenty of trivia to amaze and annoy your friends and loved ones—caution recommended on pontificating on the objects surrounding you. More importantly, though . . . they inspire us to take a second look at parts of the everyday that we've taken for granted. These are not so much lessons about the objects themselves, but opportunities for self-reflection and storytelling. They remind us that we are surrounded by a wondrous world, as long as we care to look."

John Warner, *The Chicago Tribune*

The joy of the series, of reading *Remote Control, Golf Ball, Driver's License, Drone, Silence, Glass, Refrigerator, Hotel,* and *Waste* . . . in quick succession, lies in encountering the various turns through which each of their authors has been put by his or her object . . . The object predominates, sits squarely center stage, directs the action. The object decides the genre, the chronology, and the limits of the study. Accordingly, the author has to take her cue from the *thing* she chose or that chose her. The result is a wonderfully uneven series of books, each one a *thing* unto itself."

Julian Yates, *Los Angeles Review of Books*

The Object Lessons series has a beautifully simple premise. Each book or essay centers on a specific object. This can be mundane or unexpected, humorous or politically timely. Whatever the subject, these descriptions reveal the rich worlds hidden under the surface of things."

Christine Ro, *Book Riot*

. . . a sensibility somewhere between Roland Barthes and Wes Anderson."

Simon Reynolds, author of *Retromania: Pop Culture's Addiction to Its Own Past*

OBJECT LESSONS

A book series about the hidden lives of ordinary things.

Series Editors:

Ian Bogost and Christopher Schaberg

Advisory Board:

In association with

 Georgia Tech | Center for Media Studies

BOOKS IN THE SERIES

high heel

SUMMER BRENNAN

BLOOMSBURY ACADEMIC
NEW YORK · LONDON · OXFORD · NEW DELHI · SYDNEY

BLOOMSBURY ACADEMIC
Bloomsbury Publishing Inc
1385 Broadway, New York, NY 10018, USA
50 Bedford Square, London, WC1B 3DP, UK

BLOOMSBURY, BLOOMSBURY ACADEMIC and the Diana logo
are trademarks of Bloomsbury Publishing Plc

First published in the United States of America 2019

Cover design: Alice Marwick

A catalog record for this book is available from the Library of Congress.

ISBN: PB: 978-1-5013-2599-1
ePDF: 978-1-5013-2601-1
eBook: 978-1-5013-2600-4

Series: Object Lessons

Typeset by Deanta Global Publishing Services, Chennai, India
Printed and bound in the United States of America

To find out more about our authors and books visit www.bloomsbury.com
and sign up for our newsletters.

For Emily Rose Martinez

"*I mean, what is a woman? I assure you, I do not know. I do not believe that you know.*"
—VIRGINIA WOOLF, *PROFESSIONS FOR WOMEN*

"Changes of shape, new forms, are the theme which my spirit impels me now to write."

—OVID, *METAMORPHOSES*

CONTENTS

1 THE GARDEN OF FORKING PATHS

"Then it seemed like falling into a labyrinth:
we thought we were at the finish
but our way bent round and
we found ourselves as it were
back at the beginning . . ."
—SOCRATES, PLATO'S *EUTHYDEMUS*

1

A woman runs through a forest, chased by a god.
Another attends a ball.
A third stands over a subway grate in white chiffon.
A fourth chains herself to the gates of a palace.
A fifth is carried away.
A sixth is going home now, click click click.
   (Another, not counted here, disappears in the darkness.)
A seventh approaches the guillotine.

An eighth dances backward, into cliché.

A ninth wants to stop and can't.

A tenth is furred and feathered and becomes the jungle.

An eleventh emerges from the sea.

A twelfth erases the border between countries, rides a stallion, and does the laundry, like a goddess, in a cocktail dress and black high heels.

These, my dancing princesses, of a different sort altogether.

2

I started writing this in Paris, birthplace of the stiletto, in summer. The daytime streets were crowded with women in flats, sandals, casual sneakers, and fashionable running shoes; few wore high heels. With the locals having fled to the countryside or vacations in the south, the city's annual flush of tourists was given right-of-way.

To be sure to see a woman in high heels out in the open, one had to catch her in the morning on her way to work, or else wait until the evening hours when she emerged again, doe-like, crepuscular, red lipstick refreshed. Old, young, tall, short, black, white, and everything in between, the chic *Parisiennes* filled Metro cars and twilit sidewalks; they traversed the smoky cobblestones or the chalky ground of manicured parks en route to dinners or parties, their arches lifted as if on tiptoe, moving to the street-muffled sounds of *clack clack clack clack* and *tap tap tap tap*.

3

Enter the labyrinth. Take a turn, and another turn, and another. You won't have too much time. The stopwatch is ticking, and evening is closing in. Just keep walking.

Yes, like that.

4

Our shoes pin us to the world, like Peter Pan to his shadow. More than simply facilitating our movement out-of-doors, they mediate between the wearer and the ground. Perhaps it is less the world they pin us to, but our place in it—that shadow of society that follows wherever we go.

5

In 1962, the writer and poet Sylvia Plath drew a picture of a pair of black patent leather high-heel shoes. That these were her own personal shoes is not confirmed, but I believe they were. In the drawing, done in ink, the left shoe points east while the right shoe points north by northwest, as if turned overly inward into a position that no real feet could find tenable. Above these, in pencil, Plath wrote "The Bell Jar."

6

A pair of worn shoes is a portrait of its wearer. Not just the scuffed toes and heels ground down by months or years of pavement, or the narratives told by damage and repair, but the form and function of them, their type. They are a part of our costume in both the quotidian and theatrical sense. And because the stories that shoes tell are invariably about public life, they must also be about status, and power, or the lack of it.

7

A friend of mine, a former colleague, is one of the most consistently feminine-presenting women that I know—always tastefully perfumed, always in heels. She emigrated from the Soviet Union with her family when she was just a child. Sometime during that first year in America, her father took her to a supermarket in Queens, and snapped a photo of her in front of the overstocked juice aisle. It is a picture that radiates astonishment. One might expect a look of joy to accompany that much abundance, but instead there is something closer to shock and fear in her big brown eyes. Entitlement is a learned skill.

8

Western women are often told that we're now living in a time of unprecedented choice and the ability to form our own destiny. That the world is our overstocked supermarket. *You go girl!* the advertising copy says—or seems to say. The popular narrative is that we can choose to be whatever we want to be, to work or be a "housewife," a stay-at-home mom, to have a child or to not. We're told that we can choose how we want to look, to wear makeup or not wear makeup, to grow our hair long or to buzz it off, and that we can choose whatever we want to wear on our feet. Modern shoe consumerism, especially, is often presented within the politically feminized language of *choice*. A woman's right to choose becomes "a woman's right to shoes." By this logic, it matters not so much *what* we choose, but that it is chosen. The very presence of different paths, visible but untaken, seems to indicate that choice was possible; that the path we end up on was selected as a result of our desires or, at the very least, by our personal limitations, and that this is empowerment, or even feminism. That empowerment—the taking on of power— is a matter of personal intent and actualization, rather than one of structural change. That the course we chart through the labyrinth is individual, and intentional.

Some buy it, some don't.

9

The high heels that Plath drew under the words "The Bell Jar" were meant to be an illustration for her novel of the same name. Understood to be an autobiographical *roman à clef*, it concerns a troubled young woman named Esther Greenwood at the dawn of her adult life. She is struggling to find her place in the world, beginning with an internship in New York City, and these same heels appear throughout the book as a sort of leitmotif. She is frequently aware of them, and what they are supposed to mean; the role they assign to her. The heels follow her like a shadowy familiar. We hear their origin story, bought one lunch hour at Bloomingdales "with a black patent leather belt and black patent leather pocket-book to match." At one key point in the book when she is ready to abandon her life, to unpin herself from the world, she first abandons the shoes—only to return, the stitching between self and society momentarily restored. She knows they should be a source of envy, that thousands of other college girls probably wished they could be standing in them: inside the high heels themselves, but also inside the life she has found herself in—selected for a prestigious scholarship, receiving fancy clothes, getting dressed up to attend formal luncheons and parties and to be photographed.

They are a pair of shoes she is supposed to be happy in but isn't.

10

There was a time in my own life in New York City when I wore high heels almost every day. I myself did not have much power, but I worked at the United Nations, in a place where powerful people congregate. It is a place of suits and ties, skirts and silk blouses; of long speeches and aggressive air conditioning; of *Your Excellency,* and *Madam Chairperson,* and freshly shined wingtips and yes, high heels.

I sat in rooms with presidents and royalty, although to these people I was always, precisely, nobody. There was an image in my mind of a certain kind of woman—professional, feminine, poised—that I wanted to embody. I saw these women daily, year after year, backstage to the halls of power, on benches by the ladies' room, changing in and out of comfortable and uncomfortable shoes.

11

In an early chapter of *The Bell Jar*, Esther comes across a description of a marvelous fig tree in a book, and it sends her spiraling into the daunting labyrinth of her own prospects: *I saw my life branching out before me like the green fig tree in the story,* she writes. *From the tip of every branch, like a fat purple fig, a wonderful future beckoned and winked. One fig was a husband and a happy home and children, and another fig was a famous poet and another fig was a brilliant professor, and another fig was Ee Gee, the amazing editor, and another fig was Europe and Africa and South America, and another fig was Constantin and Socrates and Attila and a pack of other lovers with queer names and offbeat professions, and another fig was an Olympic lady crew champion, and beyond and above these figs were many more figs I couldn't quite make out. I saw myself sitting in the crotch of this fig tree, starving to death, just because I couldn't make up my mind which of the figs I would choose. I wanted each and every one of them, but choosing one meant losing all the rest, and, as I sat there, unable to decide, the figs began to wrinkle and go black, and, one by one, they plopped to the ground at my feet.*

12

The shoes I saw women changing in and out of at work were a more advanced form of high heel than Plath's modest pumps, or the low kitten heels preferred by some, or the simple shoes that I could afford. These were power heels, and they were worn by women from all over the world. They were leopard print, or green and scaly. They were amaranthine and violaceous and subtly velvet. They were black and shiny as Japanese lacquer, with a shock of red on the sole. Some were plain, but uncomfortable anyway. Perhaps I have embellished them somewhat in my imagination, my memory tempered by glamour. What is not in dispute is that all of these statement shoes invariably came with a steel-spined appendage like an exclamation point: *stiletto*, the heel named for a dagger. For the women whose feet put up a fight, these shoes were changed out of and put away, smuggled in and out of the building in handbags, like weapons.

13

One warm night, outside Grand Central Station after a long day of work, I witnessed a curious metamorphosis. There was a woman standing in the shadows of 42nd Street. She was petite and nondescript, dressed in a black skirt, a black shirt, and brown moccasins, her hair pulled up in a bun. She had stopped in the middle of the sidewalk to search for something in her oversized shoulder bag. After a moment she pulled out a pair of tall, platform, silver high heels, and set them on the ground in front of her. She stepped out of one moccasin, and then the other, and into the waiting, sparkling shoes. Calf muscles flexed, legs elongated, shoulders pushed back, she pulled a pin from her hair and a dark waterfall tumbled down. Had her ankles been that narrow a moment ago? Had the slit in the back of her skirt been quite that high the whole time? The moccasins went into the bag and the woman walked away down the street and into the night, glittering, transformed.

14

When I worked in a formal office setting, high heels were never of any special interest to me beyond the fact that I liked them, and wore them, and liked wearing them. I didn't fixate. I never owned too many. If I'm honest, there were times when I liked the *idea* of wearing them more than the actual wearing of the actual shoes.

15

Walking in high heels is easy, until it isn't. YouTube is full of videos of models falling down in high heels on the catwalk, even though walking confidently in high heels is a big part of their job. The long, thin bodies wobble, then crumple like collapsing paper dolls, rising and falling several more times as they gangle their way off the stage, the spell of poise irredeemably broken. Once they fall, it seems, they are likely to keep falling. Up and down they go. They fall because they are very young, or because they are hungry, or because balance, once lost for even a moment, can be difficult to regain—or because the shoes are impractical even for a model on a catwalk. Some of the worst "high heel fail" video clips come from high heel *races*, wherein runners try to sprint while wearing tall stilettos, to earn money for charity, raise awareness for a cause, or, in the case of one Parisian event, to win free shoes for a decade from a particular company. In some instances, the runners secure the heeled shoes to their feet with packing tape. Some fall anyway. Walking in heels is one thing, but *running* in heels is a skill akin to unicycling: a thing that one can master, but that can go very wrong very quickly, even for a professional.

16

I knew a woman some years ago, a scientist, who considered herself very reasonable. She did not wear high heels. She told me once that she enjoyed the early days of spring in New York City because it was when certain young women began to venture out onto the streets wearing high heels again. And, perhaps because the women were out of practice due to the wearing of winter boots, heeled or not, this caused a degree of lurching and tripping not seen as frequently later in the summer. Perhaps the shoes of early spring were new, and not yet broken in. Or maybe it was just that the delicate bare skin of the feet had grown accustomed to tights and socks, and so chafed and then bled against the friction of plastic and leather, however familiar, making it harder to walk. The scientist told me that she liked to see the women in high heels fall down, because the choice to wear them was so stupid, and they deserved it. Maybe they would learn something, she said. I knew that the lurching and tripping women were walking like that because they were in pain; that they might have started out in the morning walking easily, but that over the course of the day their shoes had betrayed them.

17

Of course, I fell.

The last time, the worst time, I felt it happening as if in slow motion, but the realization was not enough to halt the forward momentum created by height and weight plus velocity minus balance. I was at work. I groped through air for the railing at the center of the concrete staircase I had been trying to descend, and caught it, but it was too late. A security guard and two men in dapper suits all reached out for me in gestures of futile chivalry or reflexive human kindness, but they were not standing close enough and I went down, hard.

In my defense, a few things. For one, the stairs were of a nonstandard height. I was in a terrible rush. My job required that I "dress up," and since the rest of my wardrobe was not particularly fancy, wearing high heels seemed an easy way to accomplish this. It was a warm day in September and these were the only shoes I owned at the time that seemed to fit both the weather and the occasion. They were made of real leather, and were well broken in, but I had bought them second hand, a lucky find in a thrift shop, and they were higher than I might have preferred were I given a broader choice. I was on my way to a United Nations General Assembly side event on salaries and gender equality in the developing world, when I was obliged to take a detour by the rose garden, through the esplanade of cherry trees, to a lesser-known underground passage. A shortcut. There is an art installation nearby consisting of a kind of winding ribbon of fire painted onto the paved pathway that leads out to a view of the East River. I was walking along it on my way to the underground passage—or rather, because I was trying to juggle two jobs at once, and was late, I was running. At least, I was running as much as my pair of four-inch stiletto high heels would allow.

The concrete ledge of the stairs, painted to look like a river of fire, came into perfect perpendicular contact with the exact middle of my shins. I skidded a little, more on the right side than the left, and then came to painful stillness. In no time I was surrounded by expensive wool pinstripe. The scent of good cologne. Was I okay? Did I need assistance? A radio crackled. Should they get the paramedics? *No, please, thank you, thank you so much, but I'm fine.* I was sure I was bleeding. I hobbled away into the shade of the cherry esplanade. I was wearing fitted black trousers and so could not properly assess the damage to my legs. I tried to walk on, realized I couldn't, told the security guard that I did need the paramedics after all . . . then waited a minute. I tried to walk again, found that I could, and asked the guard to cancel the call. I proceeded to the event about gender equality, but more slowly, each step painful, and with a distinct note of discord.

This was just a minor incident. It was nothing, really, though my banged-up legs hurt for months. But I was so busy that week, and preoccupied by the sharp ache in my shinbones, that it took me days to even notice the damage to my feet, or how swollen my ankles were, or the strange and tender green bruise that bloomed around the medial malleolus, that protruding bone of the ankle at the end of the tibia, which darkened into gray and blue and then, finally, purple, terminating in a wavy line of separation like a water stain on upholstered furniture.

Still, without high heels, at work I didn't feel quite put together. Like a man might feel who has forgotten to put on his necktie in a boardroom full of men in neckties. Maybe this was crazy, since not every woman where I worked even wore high heels. Samantha Power, then the US Ambassador to the United Nations, frequently dashed about the building in pantsuits and running shoes, as authoritative as anyone. Maybe I needed the Pavlovian pinched toe and lifted arch, or the strike of the heel's shaft, muted on carpet or magnified on marble, to feel fully in command of my own idea of a professional self. They made me *feel* powerful in a womanly way; suited up, compliant, like I was buckled in to the workday. Perhaps I had something to prove; or perhaps I had been made, repeatedly, to think that.

18

In the 1977 edition of *The Woman's Dress for Success Book* by John T. Molloy ("America's best-known clothing consultant tells what to wear and why!"), the introduction is titled "The Mistakes Women Make and How to Correct Them." What follows is 187 pages of advice on how to use clothes (don't dress sexy, never wear trousers, always wear high-heeled "pumps" to the office) to get male colleagues and clients to take you seriously. Then, as is often still the case now, few thought that the workplace itself might need to change, but rather that female workers must be reconfigured in order to fit into it. On the back cover there is a photo of a young woman in business attire, not smiling, with an older man standing behind her—the author himself—his hands just about to touch her shoulders.

19

Is it silly to think this much about a certain kind of shoe? To write a whole book about them? It isn't, because again and again I have found that the question of high heels—to wear them or not to wear them, what they mean or don't mean, signify or don't signify, ask for or don't ask for—has been an unlikely but fertile locus of feminist debate.

20

For better or worse, the high heel is now womankind's most public footwear. It is a shoe for events, display, performance, authority, and urbanity. We have endowed it with the power to transform, and ours is a culture obsessed with female transformation. In some settings and on some occasions, usually the most formal, it is even required. High heels are something like neckties for women, in that it can be harder to look both formal and femme without them. Women have been compelled by their employers to wear high-heeled shoes in order to attend work and work-related functions across the career spectrum, from waitresses in Las Vegas to accountants at PricewaterhouseCoopers; in places from airline cabins at 30,000 feet to seaside at the Cannes Film Festival. It's a shoe for when we're *on*, for ambition; for magazine covers, red carpets, award shows, boardrooms, courtrooms, parliament buildings, and debate lecterns.

Rather paradoxically—or maybe not—according to the 150-year-old fetish industry, it has also consistently been viewed as a shoe for sex. For women, what is the most public is also the most private, and vice versa.

Along with being our most public shoe, it is also considered the most *feminine*. Few styles in the long history of footwear have been so exclusively marked as *female* as the contemporary stiletto high heel, comparable in this way only to the lotus shoes designed for the bound feet of Imperial China. Of these two styles, the high heel is the only one still worn today. Minus the punctuated dot of the heel itself, both leave a similar tiny, triangular footprint.

21

Despite their ubiquity in the public sphere, I've often heard women like myself be criticized, even shamed, for wearing high heels. This, of course, did not sit right with me. I've also heard women defend their right to wear them as a matter of choice that has "nothing to do with men or patriarchy," and this did not sit right with me either. I do not wear them wholly peaceably because as a woman it is hard to do anything wholly peaceably in public, but nevertheless it was not until I decided to write about them that I realized how very complicated and fraught they were.

22

As for the *high* in high heels, it is easy to assume that the point of all elevated shoes is the height endowed to the wearer. As Rebecca Solnit writes in her 2000 book *Wanderlust*: *English and many other languages associate altitude, ascent, and height with power, virtue, and status.* She is writing here about mountains, but since her book is about walking, she might as well be talking about shoes, too. Solnit reminds us how inseparably we have twinned the high and the upward with the good and aspirational, so much so that one can hardly cleave the two. A "peak" is synonymous with the best of something. It is the top that dominates. We rise above our station, move up in the world, have high-minded ideas, social-climb our way into the upper classes and then look down on those beneath us. Why wouldn't it be the same with high heels?

But women's high heels of the twentieth- and early twenty-first century are not really about "height" at all. Or rather, not primarily. They are about the height *of the shoe*, not the height of the woman *in the shoe*. High heels do something to the body that is about much more than height—something that mere platforms do not accomplish. There is the flexing of legs, the displacement of hips, chest, spine, and shoulders, but something else, too.

23

"Walk as if you have two men walking behind you," my former colleague from the former Soviet Union once advised me about walking in heels. At the time, I assumed she meant that these imaginary men worked for me. Now, however, I realize that the prompt may have had less to do with pretending I was in possession of a professional entourage and more to do with something else.

24

People treated me differently when I wore high heels, in some settings better, and in some settings worse. I am already taller than average, so it wasn't height that I lacked. Maybe I simply lacked confidence. We tend to think of being tall as a good thing, but in daily life, tall women are also frequently treated like freaks. I tend to slouch—*except* when I wear high heels. As any woman whose body extends beyond the bounds of the current ideal, I'm reminded of my perceived deviance with regularity. Men frequently inform me of my own height defensively, as if it were an argument that I had started, high heels or no high heels.

25

As a younger woman, I told myself, on the advice of fashion magazines, that heels and a bit of lipstick were an easy way to look more dressed up in whatever I was wearing. They made me feel more polished in my bargain basement and consignment store work clothes. More grown up. I came of age at the height of the *Sex and the City* era, in the early 2000s. The first time I bought a pair of four-inch stiletto high heels, to attend a black-tie work event, the salesgirl gushed that I would be able to wear these particular high heels as easily with a cocktail dress as I could while shopping on a Saturday morning in a T-shirt and jeans. They were strappy and open-toed. I lived in Greenwich Village at the time, and a part of me believed her. I wanted to believe. At work, I was trying very hard to conform, to comply even; to do something to make up for or counteract the masculine allusion of my height, opinions and ambition. On some level, all performance of female culture is drag. Even as a tall woman, I *existed* for others when I wore heels in a way that I did not exist in flats. I seemed to be saying something with my shoes that pleased enough of the right people.

When you are female, with visibility comes benefit, but also consequence.

26

Men wear shoes with lifted heels on them, too. They've routinely worn footwear that is elevated at the back for over five hundred years and continue to do so. But they frequently wear sturdy heels coded as "male," which are usually about height correction, or horses: permutations of the Cuban heel or the cowboy boot. That's their masculine story, anyway, and they're sticking to it. After all, history's first true high heel—a sixteenth-century Persian men's cavalry shoe—was a grip for the stirrup.

Of course, some men wear high heels that are considered "women's shoes" as well. Being coded as female, these heels are also not really about sheer height alone, but are worn to feel or appear feminine, to dance, to impersonate women, for fun, or just for pleasure.

27

A shoe does not have a gender. Technically speaking, any high heel is a man's shoe if a man owns and wears it. As regular high heel wearer, performer, and erstwhile self-styled "executive transvestite" Eddie Izzard once quipped to an interviewer about his fashion sense, "They're not *women's* dresses. They're *my* dresses. *I* buy them." Nevertheless, high heels have often been at the center of the construction and performance of modern femininity, regardless of the sex or gender expression of the person wearing them. To deny the deep connection between womanhood and high heels is to deny the existence of culture.

28

To be feminine is not the same thing as being female. Femininity is a thing that is felt and seen, but also escaped and denied, or cultivated and proved. For trans women, non-binary or intersex individuals, and the gender fluid, high heels can sometimes play an especially important role in the expression of an inner feminine longing or recognition, particularly when access to femininity or femaleness has been previously questioned or denied, regardless of, or in concert with, the sex they were assigned at birth. Or not. Either way, high heels strike a powerful chord in the complex music of modern gender identity, with a far-reaching resonance.

29

Wherever in history they appear, from antiquity to today, elevated shoes for women have been met with the same two reactions. First, they are accepted as normal and become associated with beauty, status, and alluring femininity. Second, they are mocked and derided as vain, deceitful, frivolous, and unintelligent. These seemingly opposite but twinned cultural reactions consistently arise simultaneously, whether they pertain to the twelve-inch platforms sometimes worn by Aphrodite in the statuary of ancient Greece, or the towering stilettos found on the feet of a Silicon Valley tech entrepreneur in the 2010s.

30

Early twentieth-century suffragettes were constantly criticized for their shoes. When they wore flat shoes appropriate for marching, they were mocked as ugly and unfeminine. When they wore the more fashionable higher heeled styles of the day, they were dismissed as unserious, or as overly sexed. Much debate went into the precise, appropriate height of heels that a suffragette should wear if she wanted to be deemed both feminine and credible. The width of the heel mattered, too. You can see these precise, acceptable heels in the photographs of the day, suspended in the air on the feet of the suffragettes, as these women who wanted the right to vote were lifted off the ground by policemen and carted off to jail.

31

High heels or their predecessors have been denounced, then defended, and then denounced again, denigrated and made quasi-mandatory by the same cultures, both at the same time. No matter how you dress as a woman, turn one way in the maze and you're rewarded, turn another and you're ambushed, or trapped. It is hard not to despair when one follows this rhetoric to its logical conclusion, which is that "sensible" shoes are unfeminine, and "feminine" shoes are not sensible, therefore to be feminine is to be without sense.

We are having the same conversations about female footwear again and again, spread out over thousands of years, because the arguments are not really about fashion or culture, or even about shoes. They are political and have to do with women's role in public life.

32

When a woman attempts to assume the mantle of ultimate authority, the question of what kind of shoes she should wear can get especially complicated. During the 2016 American presidential debates, the first female nominee of a major party, Hillary Clinton, wore a pair of shoes that were no doubt the result of extreme deliberation. Flats would have been unacceptably informal for such an occasion, and so she wore heels. And yet notably high heels would have come across as too sexy and hence unserious, both for her position and her age, and so her heels were very low. They were so low, in fact, that a blocky or sturdy heel would have made them almost indistinguishable from the heels on a pair of men's dress shoes, and so to communicate her femininity, the heels were also very thin. These very low, very thin heels have a name: kitten heels. These shoes were in fact the correct, perhaps even the *only* acceptable shoe fashion choice for Clinton in these circumstances and in that moment, to show that she was at once feminine, serious, and fashionable. Being fashionable, particularly for women, is seen as a kind of social intelligence. Yet only a female candidate would find that the most acceptable sartorial choice for a presidential debate would have the word *kitten* in it.

33

Among feminists and non-feminists alike, there is no party line on high heels. As of this writing, a new high heel "controversy" seems to spring up every few months. High heels will have been banned somewhere, or required somewhere else, or some notable person will have worn them somewhere deemed inappropriate. Op-eds circulate, the Twitterati chimes in. One group will decry them as oppressive, patriarchal, or elitist, while another defends them or the person wearing them in the name of celebrating femininity, expressing culture, and safeguarding choice. (*Choice*—that word again). It seems that no matter what we choose, some valuable thing is lost. *Choosing one meant losing all the rest*. So, are high heels good? Are they bad? What do they mean? Are they feminist or anti-feminist? Do they communicate authority? Independence? Oppression? Professionalism? Confidence? Frivolity? Subservience? Sex? No one group can seem to agree.

If you ask me, the answer to all of those questions is, *yes*.

34

. . . But don't those things hurt your feet?!

Yes, high heels cause pain, and not just when you fall down in them. The good ones hurt only after you've walked in them for a fair bit, while the bad ones hurt at first contact. They chafe the skin and punish the skeleton. It is an unavoidable fact that when worn frequently, over time, they can do permanent and painful damage to the body. And, for some, high heels, and very high stiletto heels especially, have come to be associated with a certain kind of plastic, man-made woman; with Barbie feet and Ivanka Trump's brand of privileged, faux-feminist "girl power"; with the kind of Pink Empowerment that's on sale at the drug store and only costs 20 percent more than the same product in blue packaging over in the men's aisle.

35

However. Outside of this hyper-artificial realm of marketing and advertising copy, there is something deeper going on. High heels possess a complicated appeal. There is something of the *animal* in them, of the talon and the claw. (And of course, the French word for high heels is *les talons*). I am reminded of the shoe forms that appear in the gorgeous and haunting work of Dominican-American artist Firelei Baez, where, in painting after painting, the long, spiked heels seem to grow directly out of the feet themselves. Her figures, voluptuous and uncontainable, balloon and sprout and effloresce into shapes that are more wilderness than woman, oozing color, covered in tropical leaves, feathers, hair, and flowers. Instead of deciding which of Plath's anxious and tantalizing figs to choose, it is as if Baez's women have themselves become the whole tree, the whole sentient green orchard. During a significant period of her work, nearly all of her figures where feet are shown have at least one foot with a deadly heel attached, like a narrow horn, a sharpened tooth, or a stake driven into something; their feet are flexed and pointed, ready to pounce, to balance, or to dance.

36

Shoes themselves have a curious power over the imagination, long understood as stand-ins for the body and the societal self. As children, we learn through fairy tales that shoes are magical objects that can help or hinder, reward or wound, liberate or imprison. They can turn a cat into a prime minister and a serving girl into a queen. Freud described the foot as an age-old sexual symbol that occurs even in ancient mythology, and said the shoe functioned as a metaphor for the vagina. While one might do better to question which things did *not* represent the sex organs according to dear old Sigmund, this reading lends a startling cast to the classic fairy tales—to the piercing foot pain felt by the little mermaid when she steps into the world of men, or the young girl whose red shoes won't let her stop dancing even after she no longer consents, to what Cinderella may have *really* lost to the prince at the ball.

37

As the summer gave way to autumn in Paris, the wave of tourists subsided, and the streets were dominated by Parisians once more. The leaves on the horse chestnut trees turned a dusty gold-green, then mottled brown, and then drifted down one by one to the chalky ground of the manicured parks. The neon café signs seemed to come on earlier and earlier. Whatever fear or hope I may have harbored that summer that high heels had become passé was quickly banished, as the City of Light dressed up for the new season. There they were: red and velvet, or velvet-gold, or leathery green; black, brown, gray, purple, floral, paisley, white. There were spike heels and kitten heels, heels on sandals and heels on ankle boots. They were worn with dresses, slacks, skirts, shorts, jumpsuits, West African wax print ensembles, abayas, and jeans. And of course, there were flats, and oxfords, and sneakers; there were loafers and canvas slip-ons and boots and moccasins. But amidst it all, the high heel remains.

38

The story of a person's shoes is the story of her function in society, and our footprints are the marks we leave, where we've been and the direction we're going. Here, then, is the story of the most modern of women's shoes: shoes that are mythic and real, that are worn through or unblemished, that hurt or excite, that hobble or feel like flying; that are made of ice, or glass, or crystal; that we steal; that are stolen; that bleed or bear the evidence of our bleeding. Pain, pleasure, dreams, desire, status, blood: these are the refrains in the songs of women, as we strut, hobble, dance and walk through this man-made labyrinth we call the world.

2 DAPHNE IN FLIGHT, DAPHNE IN FLOWER

"For in the beginning of literature is the myth, and in the end as well."
—JORGE LUIS BORGES, *PARABLE OF CERVANTES AND THE QUIXOTE*

39

Leaves rustle on the edges of a path. A presence felt, out of sight. Twilight hovers over the tall hedges. Gravel and grass. You're not alone. You throw your weight forward onto your toes so as not to sink into the ground or become mired here.

You keep going.

40

Shoes are humankind's oldest invention to aid mobility. Thousands of years before a clever Mesopotamian first tilted a potter's wheel up onto its side to make a chariot, or a nomad tamed the first wild horse on the grasslands of the Eurasian Steppe, people have been fashioning shoes from leather or plant fiber to make it easier and less painful to get from one place to another. For the earliest humans especially, our survival depended on movement, toward prey and away from predators, for we have long been both. It is not surprising then that many of our earliest stories are concerned with flight and pursuit.

41

It is fitting that I wound up writing about high heels in Paris, even though it was another project that initially took me there, for it was in Paris that modern elevated shoes were twice born, invented and then reinvented for Western fashion as the classic high heels we recognize today. The first came in the seventeenth century at the court of King Louis XIV, when blocky *talons hauts,* inspired by Middle Eastern riding shoes, were deemed the best way for a nobleman to accentuate the muscles of his silk-stocking-clad calves and proclaim his status. The second came in the 1950s when Dior designer Roger Vivier put steel rods into the shafts of skinny stilettos, raised their height to three inches or more, and encouraged regular women to wear them in daily life. Thus, in the postwar era, when an emergency female workforce had recently been shuffled back to the kitchen, the template for the contemporary high heel made its debut.

Vivier, a Frenchman, had been making custom high heels for the likes of Josephine Baker and Queen Elizabeth II since the 1930s. He was among the first mainstream designers to push his creations to the edges of practicality and into the realm of art—of metaphor even. He was not the first to use steel in his heels, nor were his shoes the first to feature heels that were both very high and very thin. But it was his work with Dior in the 1950s that finally made the look *de rigueur*. He employed architectural flourishes. As women slowly gained a stronger foothold in the peacetime workplace and public life, the shoes deemed appropriate for such a life grew shakier. As if the thin stilettos that he championed were not precarious enough, Vivier designed heels that slanted in at an unsteady angle, called the *talon choc*, or "shocking heel," as well as the bowed "comma" heel, and heels that bent crookedly inward in a zigzag, as if buckling under the weight of their wearer. In one of his more memorable designs from 1959, he covered one of his *choc*-heeled shoes with the bright blue plumage of kingfishers.

42

From the creations of Vivier, to Manolo Blahnik, Jimmy Choo, Christian Louboutin, and Alexander McQueen, so many modern high heel designs embody ideas of metamorphosis. The fashion gods transform women into something other than human. They become plant-like, animal-like; elevated, but also easier to catch and subdue. Flowers to be gathered and collected on their tall, thin stalks. Beasts to be caught and trophied. In some of the more elaborate incarnations, employing protruding feathers and exotic hides, the wearers appear to be in the process of turning into ravens, or reptiles. There are high heels that resemble paws and hooves.

In light of this propensity for dramatic transformation, I thought at first that I would be writing primarily about shoes and feet in fairy tales: of poor Cinderella waltzing in her fragile, magical pumps, or of the twelve princesses who danced all night with enchanted men in an underground realm, their transgressions betrayed each morning by their worn-through slippers; or of the little mermaid who trades her voice for piercing foot pain so that she can walk beside a man in silence and try to make him love her. It turned out that but I had to go back even further than that, tunneling down through written literature to the proto-stories for literary fairy tales, to the likes of Ovid and his myths.

43

The original fairy tales are far darker than the cleaned-up versions we have presented to our children since Disney came on the scene. The myths that are their thematic forebears were, of course, even stranger. Before the rejected little mermaid became sea-foam, her tender new feet pained for nothing, Ovid's nymphs were being turned into fountains. Before Cinderella's dog and horse were changed into footmen to escort her to the ball, Ovid's huntress Diana was changing men into prey animals, a bachelor into a buck, as punishment for seeing her naked against her wishes. In Ovid, lovers become lions, or flowers. The bereaved become birds. People of all kinds and character become rocks, trees, streams, islands, stars. A peacock's tail feathers are the eyes of slain Argus. Juno changes Callisto into a bear for bearing her husband Jupiter a child; later, they are made into constellations, the she-bear and her hunter son.

Ovid's descriptions of these metamorphoses are graphic and physical, with each change of bodily state described in almost erotic detail. Bodies stretch, reach, shudder, and crack. Diana does not just transfigure her tormentor—she covers his flesh in a dappled buckskin and injects him with the frenzy of the hunted, changing not just his anatomy but his blood. The humans who are turned into beasts feel the spine arch forward, their hands and feet hardening into hooves, their hominal minds erased by animal panic. When they become trees, like Daphne—the nymph who is transformed into the laurel while being pursued by the god Apollo—they do so from the feet up, rooted and immobilized first and foremost.

44

I kept encountering images of Daphne all over Paris. Some days, it seemed, she was everywhere in one form or another. I found her in the sculpture halls of the Louvre, caught in mid-stride, heel up, her weight thrown forward with only the ball of her marble right foot connecting her body to solid ground. The famous Bernini statue of the same myth, housed in the Galleria Borghese in Rome, shows the horrible ecstatic moment when the hounding god first lays hands on her, her shocked mouth agape, her desperate fingers already sprouting leaves. This French Daphne, by the eighteenth-century sculptor Guillaume Coustou, is still running free, frightened but untouched. Apollo is not far off, though. Coustou's elder brother, Nicholas, sculpted her pursuer in similar fashion, and the two figures are displayed as a set, mirroring one another. I found these same Daphne and Apollo statues by the Coustou brothers reproduced in stone in the Tuileries gardens as well, trapped as if in amber on either side of a little pool beneath the horse chestnut trees. Forever pursuing, forever in flight.

One blue evening in a little English-language bookstore on the Left Bank, on a typewriter put out for customers to leave messages, I discovered that someone had typed out

all my limbs become trees

as if Daphne herself had passed through there.

But more than representations of her womanly body, Paris is full of a different allusion to the running nymph and her fate, in the form of laurel leaves.

45

In the Salle Labrouste, the great hall of the Rue de Richelieu branch of the National Library of France, one can find books and archives on art, theatre, design, and fashion. I went there to read about high heels. Built in 1870, it is like a library from a dream of libraries, with three stories of packed mahogany bookshelves along the walls, and above these, arched murals like false windows with painted treetops—the very trees found in the Tuileries—the horse chestnuts, the linden, the honey locust and London plane. And above those painted trees and their archways is a nine-part multi-domed ceiling of alabaster and deep rose, with gold, gold, gold everywhere like piping on a cake, in ribbons and swirls, rosettes and botanical flourishes, with three-dimensional gilded laurel branches and three-dimensional gilded laurel leaves. On the walls, around the edges of the great hall, are the faces, in profile relief, of famous male writers—Goethe, Racine, Cervantes, Shakespeare, Plato, Herodotus, and so on—each man marooned in a disk of shining gold beneath a flourish of gold ribbons, as if each were a medal pinned to the library's chest, ringed in garlands of still more gilded laurel leaves. Daphne, transfigured, deconstructed, splayed.

46

Daphne's main problem was her beauty, and speed was her defense. *Stubbornly single*, as Ovid put it, she roamed happily through woodland thickets with no desire for marriage, love, or sex. When Apollo sees her, he becomes fixated, intent on hunting her down to possess her. But Daphne is fast and—at least at first—can outrun the attentions of the unwelcome Olympian. Apollo is a god of poetry, healing, music, truth, and the sun, and yet in the ravishment-heavy stories of the *Metamorphoses*, even he is a predator.

He begs as he chases her, telling her to stop, saying he is no enemy, while invoking various carnivorous imagery: the wolf at the lamb, the lion at the deer, the eagle at the fluttering dove. He is none of these things, he promises, though each vivid, devouring metaphor has already been conjured. Romance as predation. It is *love* that impels him to follow her, he says, and thus she should have pity on him.

He seems bewildered that Daphne would have the nerve to reject such a good guy/god as himself at all. Clearly, she doesn't know what she is missing! *Impetuous girl*, he calls, *you have no idea who you're running from*. He expresses fear that she will fall down amid the rough terrain and scratch her "innocent legs" in the brambles. *You mustn't be hurt on account of me*, says the god chasing the terrified woman.

Daphne, in desperation, prays for her beauty to be taken away, so that Apollo will no longer desire her. But cruelly, she is robbed of everything *but* that: *She had hardly ended her prayer when a heavy numbness came over her body; her soft white bosom was ringed in a layer of bark, her hair was turned into foliage, her arms into branches. The feet that had run so nimbly were sunk into sluggish roots; her head was confined in a treetop, and all that remained was her beauty.*

She becomes the laurel tree—not just *a* laurel tree, but *all* laurel trees, *inventing* them—lovely, flowering, and of course, immobile. Once changed, Apollo presses his lips to her bark, and even her bark shrinks from his kisses. Later, she will be broken into pieces, made into crowns, and placed on the heads of imminent men by other imminent men; her leaves will be sculpted, plastered, and gilded all over Paris, on pillars and posts, columns and ceilings, threaded in the marble hair of statues. Her branches would come to signify wisdom, although her own voice has been forever stilled. Her will, her mind, have been cancelled, and her silencing beauty speaks for itself.

47

In the *Metamorphoses*, Ovid is obsessed with the flight and pursuit of women. So many of his metamorphoses take place because of women wishing to avoid men, or god-men, and the trickery it takes to overcome them. Were we only as safe as the speed at which we could run? In a book about high heels, I am sure you can guess where this is going. What better way to tame these fleeing women than to literally root them to the soil? The biggest theme in Ovid, other than metamorphosis, is rape. Jupiter rapes Io, a mortal woman, and turns her into a cow. Because Ovid's women would bear no husbands, their pursuers change them into animals and submit them to husbandry. Story after story concerns women's mobility and the impediment to that mobility, imposed on them by powers beyond their control.

48

Yes, Sylvia Plath once wrote in her journal, *my consuming desire is to mingle with road crews, sailors and soldiers, barroom regulars—to be a part of a scene, anonymous, listening, recording—all this is spoiled by the fact that I am a girl, a female always supposedly in danger of assault and battery. My consuming interest in men and their lives is often misconstrued as a desire to seduce them, or as an invitation to intimacy. Yes, God, I want to talk to everybody as deeply as I can. I want to be able to sleep in an open field, to travel west, to walk freely at night . . .*

49

A woman in motion, outside of male control, has long been viewed as a problem. In another of Ovid's stories, there is a beautiful maiden called Atalanta who could run faster than any man. An oracle warns her: *No need of a husband for you, Atalanta. Avoid all knowledge of men if you can. But you shall not escape. You will lose yourself, without losing your life.* Alarmed by this warning, Atalanta goes to live in the depths of the forest, like Daphne, unmarried. But her beauty draws a throng of admirers. Confident in her own speed, she sets a challenge to her suitors that he who can beat her in a foot race will win her hand in marriage; those that lose to her will be put to death. Finally, after she outruns a slew of men who subsequently lose their lives, Atalanta takes a shine to one of her competitors. Ambivalent about besting and hence condemning him, she lets him win, and they marry. But because the lovers do not thank Venus for their union— even going so far as to make love in one of her temples—the goddess of love changes them into lions, and once again a woman who dared to be different loses her humanity.

In some of her oldest representations, the Greek goddess of love, Aphrodite, is shown wearing tall platforms, a type of shoe whose lot is often thrown in with high heels, in character and in symbolism. Leave the battle and low platforms to Athena, and the hunt and sandals to Artemis.

The shoes found on these statues of Aphrodite were a good twelve inches in height, speaking to her status but also to her immobility, her physical passivity. She is wearing them because, at that time and in that place, they were the shoes considered the most feminine and alluring.

50

When asked what men find attractive about a woman in high heels, iconic French shoe designer Christian Louboutin, speaking to fashion photographer Garance Doré in his Parisian apartment in 2013, replied that it was the fact that the heels slowed the woman down, giving the man more time to look at her. Louboutin said nothing about aesthetics, only speed. "What is the point of wanting to run?" he said, "I am all for the pace getting slower, and high heels are very good for that."

(*Slow down, my beloved, I beg you*, Apollo calls to Daphne, *don't run so fast and I promise to slow down too.*)

51

A different Daphne—the evolutionary biologist Dr. Daphne J. Fairbairn, PhD—points out in her book *Odd Couples: Extraordinary Differences Between the Sexes in the Animal Kingdom*, that at the most fundamental cellular level of egg and sperm, across all species where sexual reproduction is practiced, it is the female component that is stationary, incapable of independent movement, and the male counterpart that is mobile.

52

Though often condemned for their impracticality, elevated shoes were first designed to serve a purpose that was very practical indeed. Eventually used by actors on the ancient Athenian stage for greater visibility, or to connote an important character, raised shoes were first made for the public bathhouses, to spare the wearer's feet from the heated floors and pools of overflown water. Their use spread throughout the Mediterranean. Men wore these bathhouse clogs, too, called *qabâqib* in Arabic. Later, they came to be associated with women especially, and were worn outside on the streets as well.

The higher and more ornate the shoe, the greater the status of the woman. Did platforms worn in the street bring to mind associations of cleanliness, as if a woman had just come from her bath? Or were they merely on a pedestal? Greek sculptures of idealized female beauty called *korai*, dating to the sixth century BCE, feature tall platform sandals. When the Moors invaded the Iberian Peninsula at the start of the eighth century, they too adopted the style.

The former Roman platform shoe industry was coopted to produce towering luxury footwear for Muslim and Christian women alike. These cork-soled Iberian shoes, called *chapínes* in Spanish, usually Anglicized to *chopines*, were often as tall as thirty centimeters. The style was later adopted by the Venetians, who made them from wood and raised them even higher, to more than fifty centimeters in some cases, and which, via trade ships in the sixteenth century, influenced shoe styles as far away as Guatemala and Japan.

Be they *qabâqib* in North Africa, *chopines* in Venice, *chapines* in Guatemala, *mitsuba geta* in Japan, or the platform *matidi* shoes of Manchu China, what had begun as a practical means to escape stepping in standing water or on a hot stone floor became an aesthetic choice, as much about the look of the artificially elongated leg as it was about the gait such shoes encouraged, or the sound made when walking in them. It would be a century more before shoe designs were widely embraced that obliged the wearer to walk with the foot not only elevated but tilted.

53

In Paris's Salle Labrouste reading room, the only unequivocally female visual representation among its host of celebrated men is at the back. There, two anonymous caryatids, statues of Grecian women some four meters high, serve as pillars with the weight of a grand archway appearing to rest on them. They are wearing drapery thin enough to reveal the swell of a nipple, their sturdy feet in sandals. Their posture is straight and their crowns branch upward into the masonry above them, like girls at a finishing school learning to walk with books balanced on their heads, except instead of books, they are balancing the whole library. These statue-women are exactly the same, a set of identical twin giants holding up the building in gesture if not reality, like goddesses in a creation myth.

It is like this all over Paris. Indeed, it is like this in many places throughout the world. In this European capital there is beauty almost everywhere you look, with statuary-men inhabiting that beauty as individuals in marble or stone or plaster, and statuary-women as anonymous, replicable ideals. Woman as decoration. Women as architecture. The statue-men are jowly, or handsome, or stout, or hook-nosed, or jolly, or stern, and some even dress visibly to the left or right in their Napoleonic statue-trousers. The men are history and inhabitant, while the women are mostly structure, environment, and landscape. You'll find women as paradigm here, too: saints and the mothers of saints, figures from myth, usually naked, like Daphne in the sculpture hall and the Tuileries, as well as the occasional queen or author. And idealized, anonymous male bodies sometimes adorn the buildings, too, especially in the more ornate sections of the Louvre. Mostly, though, there is the female body as ambiance, and the male body as individual. Similarly, living men are usually allowed to exist peaceably in their myriad humane forms, while women's bodies are more often regulated, regimented, legislated, manipulated, and subjected to the whims of design and shifting aesthetic, from her hairstyles to her footwear.

54

Beauty invades Daphne like a virus. It replaces everything else that she might have been, until she is no longer even human. *You will lose yourself, without losing your life.* To the English-speaking world, *beauty* is a load-bearing word. It is the steel in the high heel's shaft, a linguistic caryatid. It's an amorphous ideal and a disembodied virtue akin to *truth* or *love*. It's a thing that, in its purest form, will bring tears to the eyes ("It's just so beautiful"). *Handsomeness* on the other hand—that clumsy, rarely heard masculine equivalent of *beauty*—is used for almost nothing. Handsome, yes, but not handsome*ness*. A beautiful man can exist, but in being described so, he has ceded some of his masculinity.

In French, everything has a gender. The idea that a thing is beautiful or handsome and the words to express it—*belle* or *beau*, inexactly—are tangled up with and depend on the sex of the word. In the grand Salle Labrouste festooned with golden laurel, the statues, gilding, murals, windows, and chairs are female, while the books, pillars, ceiling, floor, desks, and plaster busts are male. A landscape is masculine, and so the male beauty word is used to describe it—*le beau paysage*. A symphony is feminine, and so the female beauty word is used—*la belle symphonie*. In genderless English, a landscape or a symphony or a sunset is *beautiful*. They are not "handsome." If they are described that way, it is by someone trying to be different. *Beautiful* means something that *handsome* won't stretch to cover.

55

The word *handsome*, having to do with hands or handling, came from Middle English and meant useful, apt, or clever. These are not really physical descriptors at all, unless a thing's usefulness can be read in its appearance. The word *handsome* speaks of quality and of wealth: one is paid handsomely. Therefore, even when we praise men's appearance in English, linguistically we are praising their utility. Beauty, on the other hand, is far more abstract. It is a word at once lighter and infinitely more demanding. More often than not, the burden of beauty falls on the heads, or under the feet, of women.

56

Why do we find certain shapes appealing when applied to the female body? The swell of a breast, the cinch of a waist, the arch of a foot in a high-heeled shoe. Many argue that beauty is a biological rule; a law of nature, like gravity, or the boiling point of water.

As a child, I saw an old educational Donald Duck cartoon from the 1950s called *Donald in Mathemagic Land*. It is about the beauty of mathematics and, more strikingly, the supposed mathematics of beauty. It features the familiar pants-less waterfowl dressed in a safari outfit and is narrated by a disembodied male voice calling itself "the true spirit of adventure." After illustrating some of the basic mathematics of music, the cartoon goes on to explain the geometry behind the pentagram and golden ratio, as expressed in the golden rectangle and the golden spiral. The golden spiral in particular is shown in plants and in sea life—the nautilus, the pinecone, and certain flowers. And, incidentally, the initial curve of the golden spiral would fit perfectly under the arch of a four-inch stiletto high heel.

The True Spirit of Adventure tells us that these mathematical "laws" of beauty are found in Greek architecture like the Parthenon, and that the same "golden proportions" govern the physiology of Greek statues and famous European works of art and architecture, like the Mona Lisa, the Venus de Milo, and Notre Dame cathedral—beauty's high-brow greatest hits. In a series of overlaid lines and collapsing rectangles, the True Spirit of Adventure also applies the "ideal proportions" to the United Nations building in Manhattan, and then, finally, to a woman in tights and a leotard—*but only once she rises up onto her tiptoes*. It is like this, with her heels raised, that she fits neatly into this imaginary series of unfolding boxes.

"Boy oh boy!" exclaims Donald Duck as he regards the attractive tiptoed woman. "This is mathematics? I like mathematics!"

57

Math is certainly beautiful, but is beauty mathematical? While it's true that the golden ratio can be found in some natural forms and patterns, Euclid himself never claimed the ratio had any special aesthetic qualities. This claim of aesthetic superiority was first made by the nineteenth-century experimental psychologist Gustav Theodor Fechner. Mathematicians today have said the idea that the golden ratio is a natural blueprint for beauty is "pseudo-science," "hocus pocus," and "the myth that refuses to go away."

There was something of an international uproar in 2015 when the Smithsonian put up a stall at the National Math Festival in Washington, DC, with visual aids claiming that the golden ratio could be found throughout the human body. Visitors were invited to put their face through an oval in order to see whether they measured up to the "divine proportions." In a write-up of the kerfuffle in the London newspaper the *Independent*, "appalled" mathematicians scornfully dismissed the idea of the golden ratio as an arbiter of beauty. As counterpoint, the reporter also interviewed "a believer," a plastic surgeon, who defended it. The plastic surgeon went on to say that Marilyn Monroe's face was "not perfect" but "pretty close" when it came to meeting beauty ideals supposedly derived from the golden ratio, whereas Audrey Hepburn's face did conform and therefore *was* "perfect."

Perfection, that obscure object of our desire. What the golden ratio *does* do, according to a science article in the *New York Times* that same year, is describe "a specific relationship between . . . [an] object and its parts."

Through math as well as through biology, or at least evolutionary theory, people—but especially men of the twentieth and early twenty-first centuries—have long attempted to prove that female beauty is a law of science, as unchangeable as Euclidian geometry or the ratio of notes on a musical scale. They want to understand the relationship between the object and her parts. But the golden ratio doesn't really make sense when applied to shapes that aren't rectangles or spirals, which is pretty much any part of the human body. Its placement over such forms can only be done with a degree of arbitrariness. Our obsession with the geometric nature of human beauty arose not with the advent of the mathematical concepts marshaled retroactively to support it, but rather with the proliferation and distribution of two-dimensional imagery at the middle of the nineteenth century. They fit not so much the rules of beauty, but our modern, mass-produced, flattened imagining of it, that came to prominence after the Industrial Revolution in the age of phrenology and, later, eugenics. Processed beauty. Measured, ruled beauty. Commodified beauty. Not quite apolitical beauty. Still, scientists continue to try and unlock the secrets of female beauty through geometry and biology rather than culture.

58

Beginning in the mid-1990s, researchers became preoccupied with studying women's "attractiveness" as expressed in the ratio of waist to hip. It should be noted that all of these studies were done using people assessing two-dimensional images of strangers. (Two-dimensional imagery is not where actual sex happens.) None of the studies looked at which women were able to attract the highest number of prospective sexual or romantic partners in real life, or the efficacy of her fertility.

There have been a slew of scientific studies seeking to determine whether high heels really make women more attractive or not—that is, do they increase beauty? Generally, the studies have concluded that they do. Some are concerned with why this is, but most are not. In 2014, a group of French researchers led by Nicolas Guéguen, a professor at the University of Southern Brittany, stationed a 19-year-old woman with a clipboard outside the entrance to a store, and recorded the percentage of men who were willing to engage with her for a survey about "gender issues," based on the height of her heels. When the woman wore flat shoes, the study found, 47 percent of the men were willing to take the survey. When she wore "medium heels," 63 percent of the men agreed to take the survey. When the woman changed into a pair of very high heels, a full 83 percent of the men opted to engage with her. Thus, Guéguen and his colleagues concluded high heels make women "more attractive."

The French study did not address why men might be more willing to take a survey from a teenager they were "attracted" to, rather than from one with less presumed sexual appeal. Nor did it consider if the high heels could have indicated the young woman's professionalism via sartorial formality, or even her social class, rather than her sexual attractiveness. Or, if the topic of the survey ("gender") influenced the men in what type of woman they were willing to talk to, as opposed to a survey about, say, foie gras, or football. Perhaps it was assumed that if a man was willing to talk to a woman, it must be because he desired her.

In 2012 a British research team, led by Paul Morris of Portsmouth University in Hampshire, recorded the way women walked in heeled shoes of varying heights. They found that high heels exaggerated what they called "a female gait," thus making them more sexually attractive to men. Morris and his team categorized the wearing of high heels by women as "supernormal stimuli," akin to when animals or insects attempt to attack or mate with inanimate objects that mimic triggers of attraction or violence in their own species' physiology, even when the thing doing the mimicking had crossed over the line of verisimilitude into abstraction, or even farce.

59

A tufted chest of fine white feathers or a black back covered in silvery hair. A protruding pink behind like a swollen valentine. The plane of a woman's foot tilted upward to add length to the leg, or the sway of her hips when she walks. What is beauty, and what is it for? In a human world before Shakespeare and Ovid and statues of women holding up the arches of libraries, how did we decide what is beautiful, and what isn't?

There have been as many studies, if not more, aimed at finding out what makes women's bodies sexually desirable to men as there have been on how non-male bodies fall ill and how to cure them. Most of the theories put forth are pure conjecture, and a creative or determined mind can come up with a theory to explain whatever look is currently fashionable. Even if the majority in a sampling of men *do* prefer a certain ratio of waist to hip in women, it is not actually related to her ability to conceive or bear children.

Many try to argue that certain body types, or "symmetry," are indicators of health and reproductive fitness, framing sexual attraction as a noble, logical—if subconscious—scientific impulse. But this is frequently not only scientifically inaccurate, but racist in practice, elevating particular Eurocentric features and body types as superior to others.

All of these studies trying to find the biological or geometric logic of human beauty, with or without high heels, are doomed to fail. Fittingly, they can only scratch the surface, offering a superficial snapshot of passing cultural preferences that have already become ingrained.

In her 1990 book *The Beauty Myth*, Naomi Wolf writes, *The qualities that a given period calls beautiful in women are merely symbols of the female behavior that that period considers desirable: The beauty myth is always actually prescribing behavior and not appearance.*

The beauty celebrated in popular culture cannot therefore be explained by geometry or the biological sciences because it does not indicate true biological or even reproductive fitness. Rather, the utility that beauty claims to broadcast is not a biological utility, but a social one.

60

Because women are generally smaller than men in stature, smallness—that is, thinness, daintiness, delicacy, and sometimes shortness—has frequently been taken as a signifier of human femininity and hence, beauty; so has softness, roundness and fat, which are also characteristics more commonly found in female bodies than in male ones, and so different societies have, at different times, celebrated these traits instead of smallness, or alongside it. Depending on which stereotypes of polar femininity one has decided to tease out (with maleness as its opposite), a woman with a very small body and a woman with a very large, fat body could both be seen as embodying feminine ideals, though of course there are plenty of fat, small, and round men, and muscular, tall, lean women. Averages have atrophied into metaphor, and our ideas of gender have grown dependent on an exaggeration of contrast that extends beyond the reality of human sexual difference, what is called gender dimorphism.

61

An overwhelming majority of animals spend most of their adult lives as either male or female. This is not the case for many species, nor for certain individuals within a species—including, in important ways, our own—but it *is* the dominant system. When animals reproduce sexually, it is called *dioecy*, wherein there is a male role and a female role to be played, biologically, with some version of egg and sperm.

When the males and females of a dioecious species look very different from one another, beyond just the sex organs, it usually indicates a division of reproductive effort. As biologist Dr. Daphne J. Fairbairn writes, *the division of reproductive function between males and females is almost always associated with visible differences in morphology between the sexes.* That is to say, the more different they look, the more different will be the labor involved for reproduction. The less gender dimorphism found within a species, the more likely it is that the males and females of that species will have an egalitarian relationship, where force is not used in copulation, and childrearing duties are shared.

Some of the most equal romantic partnerships in the animal kingdom can be found among colony seabirds, with the penguin, the puffin, and the albatross. In each instance, both partners look the same. Emperor penguins, for example, are not sexually dimorphic. The males and females resemble one another and are roughly the same size, although males are slightly heavier than females. They share harmonious relationships of mutual effort, even if their tasks are not identical. In heterosexual penguin courtship, it is usually the male's role to broadcast availability and the female's role to seek out and select a mate, but they share the responsibility of incubating, feeding, and raising that year's progeny. Same-sex penguin couples have been observed enacting similar mating patterns and will sometimes take eggs from male-female penguin parents to hatch as their own.

In primates, on the other hand, pronounced sexual dimorphism is common. Male gorillas often weigh twice as much as female gorillas, and a gorilla troop usually consists of one adult male and several adult females who are under his reproductive aegis. Without a mature silverback alpha male to protect them, young gorillas are vulnerable to infanticide by other adult males. The silverback makes all decisions for the group and does not take care of the young, although he is responsible for his group's safety. The males sometimes force mating on females, while the females protest both vocally and physically. Whether or not you want to call this *rape* depends on how comfortable you are with ascribing human social phenomena to the animal world. With orangutans, too, the males are much larger and stronger than the females, and thus the males make the decisions, frequently including about when and with whom sex will occur, regardless of the wishes of the female.

When the males and females of a primate species are closer in size and appearance, things can get more complicated. Male chimpanzees are only slightly larger than female chimpanzees, but their society is nevertheless male dominated, though less violently so than with gorillas or orangutans. Bonobos, on the other hand, sometimes called pygmy chimpanzees, also have males that are slightly larger than females, but their society is described as matriarchal. This has largely been attributed to the fact that the bonobo females have been able to form alliances with one another and frequently dominate the males, as a group. What they lack somewhat in physical strength they make up for in teamwork—employing social technology. Rather than forcing copulation on the females, male bonobos instead spend a lot of time with the females in the hopes that they will choose to mate with them. (And they do. Bonobos are a species without concepts of sexual ownership or homosexual stigma.)

62

In our natural state, human beings are only slightly sexually dimorphic. We live in vast colonies, like seabirds, and unlike any other large mammal. Pound for pound, male versus female, we're not too different from chimpanzees and bonobos, our closest evolutionary cousins. Men tend to be bigger, heavier, faster, and stronger than women, and usually have significantly more facial hair and slightly more body hair. However, unlike nearly every other sexually size-dimorphic species, human sexual size difference has enormous overlap. Although males are, on average, 5 inches taller than women (about an 8 percent size difference), only 9 percent of men are taller than the tallest woman, while only 5 percent of women are shorter than the shortest man. We are, in fact, somewhat *less* sexually dimorphic on all fronts than would be expected for a primate of our size. But what is perhaps most interesting when it comes to humans, gender, and external attraction, is that we may be the only species that actively seeks to exaggerate our biological differences in sex.

Fairbairn writes, *Although our sexual differences are only modest when placed on the scale of animal diversity, we are acutely aware of them in our own lives, and our sex or gender is likely to influence our cultural and social interactions as much or more than it influences our biology. Often our basic biological differences are reinforced and exaggerated by our culture so that even minor, average differences are treated as though they are fixed, dichotomous traits. This does not reflect biological reality.*

We are big fans of supernormal stimuli. Through culture—that is, style, fashion, and grooming—most human societies have sought to make men and women appear more physically sexually dimorphic than we actually are. Women are expected to have more hair in some places, and much less or even no hair in other places where hair naturally grows. Throughout history, women's clothes have been designed to alter the shapes of our bodies in ways far more severe than the clothes designed for men, marking a clear gender difference. In modern times, as the gap between men's and women's clothes have narrowed, the gap between strictly men's and strictly women's shoe styles have only widened, so that women wearing the most womanly of women's shoes are expected to appear as if they have dramatically smaller feet than their male counterparts.

Usually, these cultural alterations to women's bodies seek to make them smaller, frailer, weaker, slower, more youthful, and more encumbered. By accident or design, women's fashions and cultural condition have long served to slow us down and make us easier to dominate. Culturally, we like to masquerade as a more violent, patriarchal species of ape than our physiology would indicate. Rather than following our biological destiny based on sex difference, according to Dr. Fairbairn, we are, in fact, defying it.

63

Before the advent of what we like to call civilization, brute force was the order of the day: He who was physically strongest won. Then "strength" was expanded to mean a harvesting of resources, and the ability to delegate the use of brute force to agents within one's control, via those resources. Now, thanks to advanced political systems like democracy and international law, and concepts like bodily autonomy, human rights, and personal property, sheer physical strength no longer entitles an individual to do or take whatever he or she wants. This has been applied to men of various physical abilities for a long time now, but the idea that this also applied to women—that these protections and rights of ownership, political participation, and physical self-determination apply to us, too, despite being, on average, 8 percent smaller—is relatively novel and still not entirely embraced.

64

Exaggerating our gendered physical differences influences social equality between men and women, or the lack of it. Thus, on a very real level, the difference been the sexes, and hence our societal gender inequality, is to a large extent artificial and constructed, designed by men to increase and maintain male dominance in a way not fully in keeping with biology, and in ways that prevent human females from devising the kinds of social technologies used by bonobo females to make up for small differences in size and speed—to even out the playing field. Seen in this light, the so-called "battle of the sexes" is less about sex, and more about evolution.

65

But look. I still want to wear dresses and high heels. I like my femininity, or what I have been acculturated to think of as "my femininity," even if it is cultural. I do not want to have to imitate a man, in behavior or in appearance, in order to have power and freedom. If I want to run, I'll put on running shoes. I like to wear makeup. I enjoy adornment. Maybe you do, too, regardless of your gender. In *Bad Feminist*, writer Roxane Gay defends such stereotypical "female" things as her love of pink, rejecting the idea that feminism must exclude the trappings of female culture. Can we claim power as women without also denigrating girliness? Can't even cultural femininity be rescued from patriarchy and its metaphors of oppression?

66

Outside of culture, what does it mean to be a woman? There is more to being female than the fact of being female. We embody (or refute) an adjective. There is femaleness as basic reproductive, biological template: the meeting of an egg's

X chromosome with a sperm's X chromosome, unaltered by syndromes, deficiencies, or mutations, that grows into a female fetus as yet untouched or acculturated by ideas of societal man or woman. Then there is femaleness as metaphor, experience, and identity—separate from and sometimes even in contrast to chromosomal karyotype or reproductive organs, which is really the embodiment of our ideas of what it means to be female in culture, history, neurochemistry, mind, body, and the indefinable fire of spirit.

"What is a woman?" Virginia Woolf once asked, saying that she did not know. The very posing of this question threatens and terrifies many people even today. They think they know where the boundaries of "female" lie, and do not want you to shift or question them.

67

The giant twin sister-statues of the Salle Labrouste are the most imposing figures in a library crowded with male authors, but women as ordinary people are not ideally expected to take up very much physical space. In centuries past, in some areas of the world and for some women, particularly in Europe during the seventeenth through nineteenth centuries, our clothing was permitted to take up some of the space that our minds and voices were mostly forbidden from inhabiting. We fitted our bodies with architecture, with metal and animal bone and stiff plant fiber, turning our bottom halves into bells or the domed ceilings of libraries. A reflection of the men to whom we answered, our fathers or husbands, the space taken up by our clothes was only partly ours. Barred from having any real wealth of our own, it was *his* wealth (whomever *he* was) that we were encouraged to display, advertise, and embody. Once planted and silenced, Daphne was permitted to spread her branches.

Of course, times have changed. Now that we are allowed at universities and in military uniforms and on bestseller lists and bylines and Congress and in research libraries—though not yet, it would appear, the American presidency—women are expected to make their bodies smaller. Thinness is perceived as a kind of achievement in itself, a form of good womanly manners. And, with high heels, we have been expected to have smaller, more exclusively feminine-looking feet. Perhaps this is in order to compensate for the extra space we now take up with our intellect and public participation. As the intellectual real estate that we occupy expands, we are increasingly encouraged to minimize our physical presence in the world—not just the space we take up with our bodies, but our footprints, or even, in some cases, at least metaphorically, how far or how quickly we are expected to travel.

68

There is a recurring, apocryphal anecdote that pops up around nearly every legendary shoe designer throughout history who has made high heels for women. In it, a wealthy patroness visits the storied cobbler of her day—the eccentric Monsieur Charpentier, shoemaker to Marie Antoinette, in 1795; the mysterious Pietro Yantorny, self-styled "most-expensive shoemaker in the world," in 1905; or Christian Dior on Paris's elegant Avenue Montaigne in 1955—and complains that the expensive shoes she has just purchased have quickly fallen apart.

"Ah," Charpentier/Yantorny/Dior is said to have replied. "I see the problem. Madam will have walked in them!"

It's a joke on both: Silly shoemaker, making shoes that can't be walked in! Silly woman, buying such impractical shoes, thinking she could walk!

69

What does it mean when shoes are not made for walking? It took me a tellingly long time to make the connection that high heels had anything to do with the larger theme of walking and basic physical mobility at all. But one cannot talk seriously about women and shoes without also talking about walking, and hence also about women and freedom. In *Wanderlust*, Rebecca Solnit reminds us that there has been more written about *how* women walk than about *where* they walk—walking as spectacle, rather than walking as experience. This is because, for most of history, women were not supposed to *have* experience, or experienc*es*. They were not supposed to wander.

In a way, it is peevish to insist on speaking about walking in conjunction with high heels, because they are not walking shoes. Women who intend to walk long distances now have plenty of other shoe styles to choose from. At least it *would* be peevish, if so many women were not expected and even obligated to walk a considerable distance in high heels anyway, whether that walking takes the form of an urban commute, a social obligation, or an unplanned retreat from a dangerous situation.

70

In her poem "Daddy," written the same year that she drew a portrait of her black patent leather pumps, Sylvia Plath begins:

> *You do not do, you do not do*
> *Any more, black shoe*
> *In which I have lived like a foot*
> *For thirty years, poor and white,*
> *Barely daring to breathe or Achoo.*

71

There is terror in the public gaze. Daphne and Atalanta, aberrations both even before their transformations, fled to the forest to avoid it. From the sequestering of wives in ancient Greece, to purdah and Sharia law, to the modern policing of famous women's bodies in Western tabloids and the bullying of women on social media, women's presence in public has more often than not been prohibited, restricted, regulated, and scrutinized. Being in public, they are assumed to be for public consumption, whether that consumption takes the form of assault or simply ridicule.

72

Throughout history, different human societies have sought to increase their own sexual dimorphism, insisting that a woman's body must be smaller, softer, rounder, fatter, thinner, more protected, have less hair, or be more passive than it naturally is. She is expected to do this in order to more fully inhabit the social position marked "female." To be acceptable, respectable—that is, worthy of respect—she must fit inside a constantly shifting, imaginary series of unfolding boxes. Men's bodies are preferred to meet certain specifications of maleness, too. But it is women's bodies that have been most often manipulated, legislated, controlled, and contorted. A number of those cultural practices have been aimed at the feet.

73

Walking is important, not just as transportation and means of escape, but as metaphor. Most of all, walking is the experience by which we orient our body and mind in relation to the world. And if walking is how we understand ourselves as minds and bodies in relation to the world, then to disrupt walking is to disrupt the relationship between self and world. In light of this, it is worth examining what the ubiquity of unmanageably high heels says about the dark dreams of our dominant culture.

74

The word *tramp*, now a little outdated in all its usages, can have very different meanings. As a verb, it means simply *to walk*. A tramp, then, means *one who walks*. But as a noun for a man, a tramp is a vagrant. As a noun for a woman, a tramp is a whore. In both of these are reflected modern ideas about class and sexual control for men and women who are seen on foot in public. By this logic, a man who walks is simply poor, whereas a woman who walks is considered amoral, and sexually indiscriminate. Streetwalker, a public woman, woman of the streets, Solnit reminds us, are all terms that mean *prostitute*. Women, and our sexuality—because a woman is often seen to *be* her sexuality—is not supposed to travel. If we do, the world says, you may be seen as belonging to whomever is able to catch you. It says it cannot be held responsible for what monstrous metamorphoses may occur.

3 ASHES, SEA-FOAM, GLASS, GOLD

"'Listen,' said the mother secretly.
'Here's a knife, and if the slipper is too tight for you,
then cut off a piece of your foot. It will hurt a bit.
But what does that matter? It will soon pass,
and one of you will become queen.'"
—THE BROTHERS GRIMM, "CINDERELLA"

"You'll keep your graceful movements;
no dancer will ever glide as you do,
but every step you take will feel like
you're treading on a sharp knife
and make your blood flow."
—HANS CHRISTIAN ANDERSEN,
"THE LITTLE MERMAID"

75

The term *fairy tale* is often used as a metaphor for a dream come true, a fantasy, a happily ever after. In the language of magazine copy, to say that something is "like a fairy tale" means that it is a moment of favorable transcendence when something is good or even perfect—especially in the context of fashion or romantic love. The fairy tale wedding, an opulent fairy tale dress—the pair of fairy tale shoes that allow you to attend an event above your social station and meet a rich, handsome prince. But the folk tale origins of fairy tales are nearly as steeped in blood, trial, and pain as the fates of the doomed mortals of mythology.

Myths like the ones Ovid retold seek to explain the world or the origin of its wonders, to describe—like the golden ratio, beauty's sham architect—the relationship between the object and its parts. They imagine the human body as progenitor of nature, rather than the other way around. Species of animals or trees, constellations of stars, and chains of islands exist because of the folly or fate of a particular man, woman, or god. Sex is often at the core of these mythic conflicts: the infidelity of god-spouses, the rape of mortals and nymphs, the lovers who choose the wrong place to make love. The very fabric of the world is changed as a result of these libidinous actions.

Folk and fairy tales, on the other hand, usually feature ordinary people as their protagonists, who are punished or rewarded within the spectrum of earthly life. They star the underdog and the disinherited, demographics that children instinctually side with, since they themselves have power over no one. Fairy tales are likely to be instructional, even if the lesson is cloaked in strangeness—part behavioral manual, part fever dream. Sex may be hinted at obliquely via marriage, but it isn't explicitly featured. Even as they encounter supernatural beings or objects, it is the human person that is the focus, and their gains reflect the desires of regular folk: marriage, children, money, status, escape. It is within the context of these human desires that the ancient stories of shoes begin.

76

Sometime around eleven to twelve hundred years ago, in a palace of the Tang Dynasty in Imperial China, a young dancing girl was encouraged to wrap her feet tightly in cloth so that they would remain small, dainty, and beautiful, while the rest of her body grew to maturity. Or maybe not. Instead of a young dancing girl, perhaps it was the king's favorite concubine, who tied up her feet so that they were shaped like little hooves, to dance with on the golden stage shaped like a lotus flower that she had built for him. Because the king liked it, the other concubines followed suit. Or, it could have been a queen born with a clubfoot, who demanded that all of the women of her court wear foot bandages as well, so that their feet would resemble hers, and she would not feel like an oddity.

There are several legends and no clear origin story to the custom of foot binding in China, though we know it was practiced at least as early as the tenth century. It began as a specialized tradition, confined to the fashionable elite ladies of the royal court, but spread to become a normal, common practice among nearly all Han Chinese women by the seventeenth century. Originally, it was meant to indicate that a woman came from a family whose wealth was great enough that she need not work, or even walk very much. Beauty as idleness. Immobility as status. The bound feet were called lotus feet, after the delicate lotus flower, and the shoes to be worn with them were called lotus shoes.

Like many indicators of status, what initially meant wealth came to mean attractiveness on its own, out of context, which all women are expected to possess, or at least to perpetually aim at, despite their social station. *Beauty*, that load-bearing, obscure object. Women who were not wealthy and still had to walk and work were eventually expected to bind their feet, too. Girls and women with bound feet not only walked on those feet, they labored alongside their families in shops, on farms, and in fields, their wrapped, bent, broken-and-healed lotus feet tucked into tiny slippers, walking shoes, and even work boots.

77

Around the same time that foot binding first appeared in the court of Imperial China, a Tang scholar named Duan

Chengshi recorded a story on a scroll in Classical Chinese about a young girl named Yexian who had very small feet. She lived with her stepmother and stepsisters, who treated her badly. Her only friend was a magical fish. One day, the stepmother kills the fish and serves it for dinner, hiding its bones under the dung heap. When Yexian discovers what has happened, she is grief stricken. While she weeps, an unknown figure materializes out of the sky and tells her that she can wish on the fish's bones and her wishes will be granted. Yexian wishes for fine clothes and is given a robe as blue as kingfisher feathers, and a pair of gold shoes that fit her perfectly.

Yexian goes to a festival dressed in her new finery, but one of her stepsisters recognizes her and she is forced to flee in haste, leaving one of her golden shoes behind. The shoe is found by a cave dweller, who then sells it to the king. The king becomes obsessed with the tiny, golden slipper. He forces every woman in the kingdom to try it on, but it is always too small. Despite being made of precious metal, it is as light as goose down, and is silent—it made no sound, not even on stone.

The shoe maddens the king. He tortures the cave dweller to try and ascertain the thing's origin, but it's no use. He orders that anyone who can wear it be taken into custody immediately. Eventually he finds Yexian, the only woman with feet small enough to wear the golden slipper. He marries her, making her his primary wife, while the stepmother and stepsisters are killed. Though the story may sound familiar, it was then the first of its kind to be written down as literature.

78

Beauty is mutable. It is the state of being aesthetically pleasing that transcends mere pleasantness. Its embodiment is ephemeral but so are its ideals. We may like to look down on what was done for beauty in the past that we no longer find beautiful now, but it's more useful to try and believe in the spell it once wove over women and men, to understand that it was just as potent as anything we might succumb to today or tomorrow. It is easy to dismiss the pain of achieving beauties past as grotesque or unnecessary once we no longer find them beautiful, less so when they still captivate us.

79

Foot binding began for nearly all Han Chinese girls between the ages of four and six. Binding the feet of younger children was not feasible because, it was explained, they could not stand the pain. If their families waited until after age six or so, it was usually too late.

There were different kinds of bindings, but the general idea was the same: the bones of the toes were broken and bent upward, back, or both in combination, and the whole foot was tightly wrapped to control and minimize growth. The bones were then continually re-broken and set over the next several years, so that girls reached womanhood with feet that had been molded and constricted into blunt little hoof-like triangles, sometimes no bigger than the front portion of a modern stiletto.

Many of the shoes for lotus feet came with a tiny fluted heel, or an internal wedged arch, to make the already manipulated feet look even smaller when shod. High heels and lotus shoes are often mentioned in contrast to each other, but in many instances they were one and the same.

80

Susan Sontag, writing on women and sickness, noted that frailty and vulnerability had increasingly become an ideal look for women. But this only holds true if the woman can maintain her charms—that is, if she can suffer and be made frail without complaining about it. Women are expected to suffer, must expect suffering, and yet must not speak of it.

"A lady never admits that her feet hurt," says Marilyn Monroe's character in the film *Gentlemen Prefer Blondes*. But why is that? Perhaps, despite its ubiquity in the female experience, expressed pain is an indication of damage, or impending damage. Like the princess in "The Princess and the Pea," but in reverse, a true lady of quality will not feel the pain inflicted on her, by herself or society, so that she can be considered feminine and beautiful. The pain belongs behind the scenes. To admit to the pain is to admit that there is a backstage to the scenery at all, that there is artifice, which is a kind of fraud. If pain means injury, and injury means damage, then because women have long been seen as part human, part commodity, the expression of pain indicates an admission that she is damaged goods, and of lowered value.

Yexian's slippers were impossibly small, but they were also silent.

81

As important as these miniature, triangular feet were for Imperial Han Chinese women, just as important were what having those feet did to the body and how it moved, which an added heel or wedge further exaggerated. The women walking on such feet had to develop extra strong muscles in the thighs and backside just to keep their balance. This kind of physique was then associated with the tiny feet in their beauty ideal. The lotus feet also necessitated an extreme halting, mincing gait, which was very different from a man's gait, walking as he did on unbroken, natural feet. This altered type of walking was deemed feminine and desirable. It is a gait not unlike that produced by a woman today walking in very high, uncomfortable heels— the feminized walk described by the British researchers as supernormal stimuli.

Often, how a woman walks in high heels has less to do with the height of the heel itself and more to do with how well the shoe is attached to her foot, and how much pain she is in. With the more extreme bound feet, however, the distinctive walk they produced was involuntary. This elicited a sort of *behavioral* gender dimorphism in addition to the change in the culturally accepted female body shape. Natural feet were considered manly, and so the natural state of the body became masculine; one had to sculpt, suffer, and reinvent to be read as female.

82

The lotus flower is a symbol of enlightenment in Buddhism and has at times been used as a sexual metaphor in Taoist texts. It's the name of a seated yoga position, and also a British sports car. Growing as it does out of the muck, it is often harnessed as an image of beauty in adversity. After her suicide, Sylvia Plath's estranged husband Ted Hughes selected an epitaph for her tombstone, taken from a Chinese poem, which read: *Even amidst fierce flames, a golden lotus is planted.* I was taught by my hippie parents in Northern California in the 1980s that "lotus" was the word for a girl's private parts. This caused years of confusion when unfamiliar adults thought they were saying "flower" or "sports car" or "sit cross-legged" or "beauty in adversity" to me, when what I heard was something else.

83

Elizabeth Semmelhack, curator of the Bata Shoe Museum in Toronto, has argued that the "high heel walk" is, at least in part, culturally constructed. Ideas about what exactly high heels do to the female body have changed over time, as have descriptions of the walk. Do high heels make women totter? Strut? Sashay? Do they make the body appear curvier, or leaner?

Much has been written about the way high heels are supposed to emphasize the breasts and buttocks, making these two words sound like they refer to cuts of meat rather than regions on a woman. Do they force a curve into the lower spine and push the ribcage open? Perhaps they *encourage*, rather than *force*. It's possible that walking in normal, well-fitting, well-secured high heels does not actually compel a person to walk any particular way at all, but rather, makes certain consciously performed walks easier or possible.

High heels *do* make the legs look longer, increasing their ratio to the rest of the body by putting more distance between where the toes touch down and the hips. Long before Western fashion allowed for trousers and short skirts on women, the high-heel-wearing men of seventeenth-century Europe discovered that a raised heel causes the muscles of the exposed calves and thighs to flex and look shapelier. They are like push-up bras for everything below the waist. As writer Mary Karr asserted in an essay about high heels for the *New Yorker*, "an elongated foot and leg just announces, *Hey, y'all, there's pussy at the other end of this.*"

84

Many versions of the Cinderella story can be found all over the world. From ancient Egypt, to medieval Korea, to the Brothers Grimm in early nineteenth-century Prussia, each version involves four key elements. The first three are as follows: a beautiful young girl in a low social position, a man in a high social position, and a lost shoe that serves to unite them. The fourth and most important element is that the girl's status is raised because the shoe has brought her to the man.

In these varying but similar Cinderella tales, sometimes there is a magical intermediary who puts the girl in front of the man, such as a fairy godmother, or the spirit of the girl's dead mother who comes back in the form of a domestic animal or a tree that rains down gifts. But not always. Sometimes it is merely a matter of circumstance that throws the girl and the man together. She is hired to be a dancing girl at the palace, or her shoe is taken by a bird and dropped into a rich man's garden. In some versions of the story, the shoe is made by the girl herself, and has been crafted or embroidered so finely that the man simply *must* meet and marry its craftswoman. Often, as with Yexian, it is the tiny size of the shoe that impresses the man, suggesting to him the bodily delicacy of its wearer in her absence. Every version of the story ends with a wedding as *deus ex machine*: The beautiful, intelligent, kind, or talented girl of low or reduced social status becomes a woman of high social status because she has been selected for marriage by a high-status man.

85

Interestingly, but perhaps not surprisingly, no stories of the opposite set-up exist. There are no fairy tales in which high-status women select attractive or clever low-status men, and certainly not because of their shoes. This may be because even high-status women were not permitted to select their own mates most of the time. While low-status men *do* frequently marry high-status women in fairy tales, the women are presented as prizes, passively offered as incentives to solve mysteries or complete heroic tasks, or as windfalls to power gained through trickery, with a wife as a signing bonus to a kingdom.

86

It is a common fairy tale theme for a character to transcend his or her station due to goodness, cleverness, beauty, or luck—notably with the help of footwear—even if he or she does not travel very far geographically. Sometimes the shoes themselves can supercharge actual movement, such as with the frequently encountered "seven-league boots" that transport the wearer a league (about three and a half miles) with each step. Mobility in hyperdrive. When shoes are mentioned at all in fairy tales, they are usually magical—or turn out to be. Or, if the shoes themselves are not magical, their function will be one of magic-like metamorphosis. Such is the case with the story "Puss in Boots."

The titular puss in "Puss in Boots" is more or less an ordinary cat, other than the fact that he is very clever and can talk. The way the story's human characters respond to him does not indicate any great surprise at these facts. He is simply a farm cat, one of the few possessions left to a miller's son after the death of his father. Dismayed by his meager prospects and limited property, the miller's son decides that he will kill the cat and skin him for his hide. But the cat manages not only to talk his master out of killing him, he gets him to agree to provide him with a fancy new pair of boots. "Then I'll be able to go out, mix with people, and help you before you know it," the cat tells him in the version told by the Brothers Grimm.

Although he is only a cat, Puss knows that he can use fashion—and footwear in particular—to maneuver social mobility for himself and the miller's son. He intends to social climb, through trickery based on appearances and false reputation, and it all starts by raising his own station with an ordinary and non-magical pair of shoes. With these, he is able to present his master as someone already rich, thus making it easier for him to gain more wealth, as well as the interest and trust of the wealthy. By the end of the story the miller's son has married a princess, become king, and has appointed the booted cat as his prime minister.

87

Shoes play a very different role for fairy tale females than they do for fairy tale males. Men's folkloric footwear is usually an instant boost to power, be it magical or merely social, whereas with women it is much more complicated. Fairy tale shoes for women and girls are often correctional, if not dangerous, or serve as stand-ins for her character or worth. As mentioned above, one of the oldest and most widely told of these tales can be boiled down to the girl who married a prince because of a shoe.

In fairy and folk tales of all stripes, from all over the globe, shoes have been used to represent the movement from one place to another, and hence ideas of advancement, liberty, and hope—or conversely, of death and punishment for the wicked. They represent transit. They facilitate liminality.

If shoes are so central to ideas of action and advancement, what does it mean if a culture imagines that an ideal shoe for women is one that inhibits her movement, like the lotus shoe or the high heel? But while lotus shoes, high heels, and other culturally feminized footwear may inhibit *physical* movement, it is important to remember that there are other kinds of mobility to consider.

The landscape that women are more often expected to traverse, where they can find their gains and progress, is within the abstracted landscape of male desire, and the windfalls to its worldly consequence.

88

The idea of a glass slipper was first introduced to the Cinderella story in seventeenth-century France by the author Charles Perrault. There are no high heels in fairy tales, or at least not explicitly, unless one can conclude that Perrault's *"Cendrillon"* ("Cinderella") was set in his own country and time—the reign of Louis XIV—in which case the original glass slippers, or *pantoufles de verre*, like their twentieth century and early twenty-first-century Disney counterparts, were indeed imagined as high heels.

Perrault was interested in folk tales, fashion, and labyrinths. A secretary to the king's finance minister, he used his influence to procure a contract for his brother to design a new section of the Louvre (itself a kind of labyrinth), beating out the famous sculptor Bernini, of *Apollo and Daphne* fame, with whom Perrault had a difficult relationship. At the age of forty-one, he advised Louis XIV on the addition of thirty-nine fountains to the labyrinth at Versailles, each representing one of Aesop's fables. He became a member of the Académie Française, and later produced an illustrated guidebook printed by the royal press, called *Labyrinthe de Versailles*, in 1677. In his sixties, after retiring from his secretarial post, he turned to writing the fairy tales for which he is now best known, most notably "Sleeping Beauty," "Little Red Riding Hood," "Cinderella," and "Puss in Boots"—all inspired by older fables. In 1697 he published *Histoires ou*

Contes du Temps passé: Les Contes de ma Mère l'Oye (*Tales and Stories of the Past with Morals: Tales of Mother Goose*).

89

In much the same way that the towering *chopines* of Europe influenced the shoe styles of the colonial Americas and the Far East via Venetian maritime trade routes, the appearance of high heels in Europe corresponded with the establishment of overland trade routes across what is now Iran, by English merchants wishing to avoid the hostile Ottomans. The Persians wanted English wool, while the English wanted carpets and other Persian luxuries. These new commercial corridors also increased the flow of grain, fur, and timber from Russia and Poland, and the Persian cavalry style of knee-length robes and riding shoes with a thick heel were adapted by the Polish cavalry, too. This militant, equestrian shoe style then seeped into mainstream European men's fashion from two directions, north and east, so that by the early seventeenth century, glamorous heeled riding boots and elegant heeled court shoes were commonplace throughout the palaces of Europe.

By the middle of the seventeenth century, when heeled shoes had spread beyond the court, the newly crowned King Louis XIV decreed that his nobles—and no one else—would wear heels covered in red silk. When his great-grandson, King Louis XV, took the throne, he too wore red-heeled shoes, as did *his* successor, his son King Louis XVI, who, at age fifteen, married the fourteen-year-old Marie Antoinette in 1770; these thick *talon rouge* were described in *Le Costume Français* of 1776 as "the mark of the nobility [that shows] they are always ready to crush the enemies of the state at their feet." In other words, the red represented the blood of the vanquished.

High heels debuted in the West as a masculine, even violent symbol of military might and intercontinental economic expansion. In time, though, high heels made their way onto women's feet, too. When Marie Antoinette was guillotined in 1793, at the age of 37, her final words were *Pardon me, sir, I didn't mean to do it.* She had accidentally stepped on her executioner's foot with her red leather high-heeled shoe, which she had saved in her cell and kept pristine for the occasion. High heels for both women and men went out of fashion not long after, and did not return to the streets of Paris again until the 1850s.

During Perrault's era, the kind of shoes that a woman would wear to meet royalty were usually made with a heel that tapered slightly in the middle, sometimes called a "spool heel," of two or three inches in height. One hundred and fifty years later, the Brothers Grimm would write their own Cinderella (or "Aschenputtel") into a pair of slippers made of silver on the first night of the ball, then gold for the second, like Yexian. But the glass version would prove the most fertile to the modern Western imagination. Perhaps there was simply something irresistible about the image of a woman dancing with unbroken glass underfoot, like her own Jewish wedding waiting to happen. It added an element of danger and improbability not present when their materials were merely precious.

90

In the Brothers Grimm version of Cinderella, the stepsisters are not ugly. They are beautiful of feature but possess "proud, nasty, and wicked hearts." With this description comes an important aspect of the Grimm tale, which is beating out female competition. But like the Han women of Imperial China, the stepsisters are obliged to violently alter the natural state of their feet in order to be found marriageable, when their mother encourages them to cut off either their heels or toes to fit into the impossibly tiny shoe made for Cinderella.

Yes, it will hurt, they are told, but so what? What is a little bit of excruciating pain when there is a prince at the door? The prince in question is especially dim in the Grimm version, and is ready to take away and marry each of the stepsisters in turn, once they manage to stuff their mangled feet into the slipper—until the blood pooling there, a different kind of *talon rouge*, is pointed out to him by some talking birds.

The prince looked down and saw that the stockings of the bride were colored red and that her blood was streaming out of her slipper, the Grimms write. In their version, the prince only recognizes Cinderella's face—which has been right in front of him the whole time—once she puts on the golden slipper. Without her delicate shoe, as far as the prince is concerned, she is not herself.

91

In *Howl*, the poet Allen Ginsberg writes, *I saw the best minds of my generation destroyed by madness, starving hysterical naked . . . who walked all night with their shoes full of blood on the snowbank docks waiting for a door in the East River to open.*

92

Blood pools in the black patent leather high heels of Esther Greenwood in *The Bell Jar* too. Not once, but twice. The first time it happens, Esther drops a razor blade onto her leg from above, with enough momentum to cut rather than graze. *Like a guillotine*, Plath writes. *I felt nothing. Then I felt a small, deep thrill, and a bright seam of red welled up at the lip of the slash. The blood gathered darkly, like fruit, and rolled down my ankle into the cup of my black patent leather shoe.* A similar thing occurs after she has her first sexual experience, and inexplicably starts to hemorrhage, the blood once again collecting in the shiny black leather, bloodying her feet, like the vanquishing French aristocracy, or Ginsberg's best minds, or the vanquished stepsisters.

(You do not do, you do not do
Any more, black shoe
In which I have lived like a foot . . .)

93

In much the same way that feminized shoes have historically served to inhibit women's movement as a sign of social class—to keep her confined to the palace or the house, guarded and precious—the removal of the female foot from the ground altogether is another way that cultures have accomplished this. There is a recurring idea that a woman's contact with the street, with society, and with the public world, makes her impure.

In Nepal today, there are little girls whose feet are never permitted to touch the ground. This is because they are thought to embody the spirit of a real, living goddess. Called *Kumari*, these goddess-children are selected from a certain social caste, that of silver- and goldsmiths, around the age of three or four. It is done through a mysterious and intuitive process that takes place in a dark room. To be eligible, a potential Kumari must have never shed blood or been afflicted by any disease. She must retain all of her baby teeth and must possess "the thirty-two perfections of the goddess," including black hair, black eyes, eyelashes like a cow, thighs like a deer, and a voice "as soft and clear as a duck's." Once selected, she is worshipped and petitioned for blessings. Her feet are painted red and covered in flower petals. During her tenure, her feet must never once touch the ground. She must never wear shoes, and if her feet must be covered, it will be with blood-red stockings. Shoeless, above the ground, she is outside society. When she experiences her first menstruation, it is believed, the goddess vacates her body. Only then can she walk outside again and live a normal life.

As of this writing, the current Kumari of Kathmandu, who is attended to by her older sister, loves to hear the stories of princesses in Western fairy tales read aloud to her, and passes her time as a living goddess listening to "Snow White," "Beauty and the Beast," and "Cinderella."

94

Bound feet were painful, but they were also beautiful, because society decided it was so. The pain was worth it because beauty *was* worth. As a woman, the more beautiful you were, the more worth you had. Beauty was pain and pain beauty. A Han woman without bound feet in Imperial China was considered ugly and unmarriageable, and to get married and come under the legal and sexual aegis of a man was then, and continues to be, the primary expectation of women worldwide.

Perceiving oneself to be beautiful, and the sense of power or safety that it provides, is its own kind of spectatoring pleasure—even if it is a "pleasure" one has to grit one's teeth through. *Plus ça change*, etc. We see ourselves through the eyes of society, through the eyes of men or women who may desire or judge us, and find that we conform. These norms bleed across the edges of heterosexuality, too. *Even pretending you aren't catering to male fantasies is a male fantasy*, Margaret Atwood writes: *pretending you're unseen, pretending you have a life of your own, that you can wash your feet and comb your hair unconscious of the ever-present watcher peering through the keyhole, peering through the keyhole in your own head, if nowhere else. You are a woman with a man inside watching a woman. You are your own voyeur.*

95

No matter what a straight woman in America may accomplish in her professional life, unless she has a husband and at least one child she does not "have it all." This "having" of the "all" (job, spouse, progeny) is a state of being that most men are expected to take for granted, to resist, even, and yet is still considered to be a sort of modern fairy tale for women. Through popular culture, notably the Disney Princess Industrial Complex—which has even reached all the way to the little sequestered living goddesses of Kathmandu— we train girls from a young age to look forward to that someday when their prince will come, the tiny shoe will fit, and their happily-ever-after will begin. The emphasis on this heteronormative ideal has not eased up despite the additional expectation of a career.

96

Regardless of the type of shoe featured, fairy tale shoes can often take on strange meaning, such as the pairs worn out night after night by the twelve princesses in "The Worn-Out Dancing Shoes," also called "The Twelve Dancing Princesses." It is a story about women's secrets, and of shoes telling tales. Cinderella and Yexian are helped by their shoes, but many versions of fairy tale footwear do worse than tattle on their wearer.

At the end of the Brothers Grimm version of "Snow White" ("Little Snow White"), the evil queen is made to wear shoes of hot iron and is forced to dance in them until she dies—at her daughter's wedding, no less. This makes more sense when one considers the extremely morbid nature of the Grimms' prince himself, who does not meet Snow White until after she has eaten the poisoned apple and the dwarves think she is dead. He is simply passing by the funereal spectacle in the forest when he sees what he believes to be a beautiful dead woman and offers to buy her corpse. He then takes her body back to his palace and makes his servants carry it around from room to room, so that he can always be near to her. It isn't true love's kiss that brings the Grimms' Snow White back to life, but rather the annoyed jolting of an angry servant who, tired of lugging the supposed dead body of a teenager around the castle, accidentally dislodges the piece of apple and restores her to life. It is little surprise, then, that this pair decide to execute the wicked mother of the bride as wedding entertainment.

97

While many fairy tales—"Snow White," "Beauty and the Beast," "Cinderella"—have ancient origins, others have far more modern roots. Take, for example, the oeuvre of the eccentric Danish writer Hans Christian Andersen. While some of his creations, like "The Little Mermaid," draw on older and more traditional tales, other of his works were completely original to the nineteenth century, even though we have come to think of them in the same breath as older fables.

Such was the case with Andersen's "The Red Shoes," about a young girl named Karen who sees a pair of shoes in a cobbler's shop and becomes fixated on wearing them to a village dance. But the shoes, described by some as being possessed by the devil, have a mind of their own. Once she puts them on, she cannot take them off again, and the shoes take control.

What often gets forgotten when discussing Andersen's tale of the deadly dancing shoes is just how young Karen is. In the story, she has her first communion, which usually happens when one is in the second grade. She's a little girl, not even an adolescent, and yet the story is and should be read as a parable of sexual promiscuity, whatever Andersen's conscious intentions may have been.

The lesson of the red shoes is distinctly female. Although Karen may have wanted to begin dancing, once she starts, she is no longer in control of when she can stop. A desire that felt simple to her quickly gets away from her, and spirals into catastrophe, bringing her to dark and dangerous places.

She put on the red shoes, Anderson writes. *Why shouldn't she? And then she went to the ball and began to dance. . . . But when she wanted to turn right, the shoes danced to the left, and when she wanted to move up the floor, the shoes danced down the floor, down the stairs, along the street, and out the town gate. Dance she did, and dance she must, right out into the dark forest.*

Once she gives an initial *yes*, she is no longer allowed to say *no*. She wanted to dance, just not like this, but a *yes* is an unmitigated *yes* forever. Eventually, the town executioner takes an ax to her ankles, and the shoes go dancing away with her severed feet still inside of them. Karen is considered wicked for wanting to wear the shoes in the first place, which were made for a girl of a higher social rank. She finally dies, a crippled amputee, atoning for her sins in the church where once she flaunted her shiny new red shoes for Sunday service.

98

Historically, high heels have been seen as bad for women physically, but also morally. During the Jazz Age, raised hemlines suddenly put women's shoes on display in a way they had not been when partly hidden under long Victorian and Edwardian skirts. Many of the designs were the same as they had been for evening shoes thirty years earlier, at least in terms of the height of the heel, but socially conservative critics still blamed high heels for the perceived impropriety of the Flappers wearing them, and petitioned companies to cease their production. In the early twentieth century, high heel "abolitionists" even went so far as to call for the imprisonment of their manufacturers "on the ground of mayhem and mutilation."

Legitimate claims that certain shoes were damaging to the body were blurred with the idea that they would also damage the virginal, obedient female soul. Because of this, there exists a complicated problem wherein high heels have become connected with sex, and hence liberty and modernity, which makes dismissing or critiquing them look regressive and puritanical.

Heels are lustful, supposedly inspiring lust in both the wearer for the shoe, and in the observer for the wearer. (And, in a way, the lust of the wearer for the shoe may in fact be a mirrored longing to be a lusted-after wearer. *You are a woman with a man inside watching a woman.*) Mary Karr writes of her high heel habit, *I was a slave to the desire that rules our libidinal culture.* High heels have so successfully been cast as a kind of *excess*, like booze and sex, in a culture in wary awe of excess, that to condemn them can come off as prudish. The pain they cause has been reframed as sin, but the kind that you want: sinful like chocolate, or an ill-advised tryst. A guilty pleasure. The mayhem without the mutilation. They walk the sometimes-delicate line between *fuck me* and *fuck you*.

It's not very cool to talk about that fact that high heels are painful. It spoils the illusion. A true princess will feel the pea under a pile of mattresses, but not her Jimmy Choos. Myths of class come into play here, too. With the rise of designer status heels in the late twentieth century, when a single pair of luxury stilettos could suddenly reach into the four figures, the notion was put forward that *expensive* high heels did not hurt in the same way that cheap ones did. The pain was an issue of quality and engineering, not of concept, or so the argument went. If your feet hurt in high heels, by this logic, it was because you couldn't afford otherwise. The pricey shoes of Manolo Blahnik especially were often proclaimed to be "as wearable as they are exquisite." Cue Sarah Jessica Parker as Carrie Bradshaw in *Sex and the City*, dashing all over Manhattan in her beloved, towering *talons*.

As an owner of such shoes, I can tell you that this is, at best, a lie. But at $400 a pair, few women could afford to find out whether or not this was true. (I can't even afford it; I bought mine gently worn on eBay.) Perhaps the number-one piece of advice in John T. Molloy's 1977 *The Woman's Dress for Success Book* was that a woman should wear the most expensive or expensive-looking clothes that she possibly can; while there *is* some truth to the idea that a well-made shoe will be much less painful than a poorly constructed one of the same height, it does not take away the inherent pain or difficulty of the design. Still, this notion added a further dimension of social class to Marilyn Monroe's advice in *Gentlemen Prefer Blondes* that a lady must never complain of foot pain. Not only is it un-ladylike to admit that your feet hurt in your stilettos—it makes you sound cheap.

99

Silence, pained feet, and difficult tasks performed at a handicap are common fairy tale themes, including in the most beloved of Andersen's stories, "The Little Mermaid." Like "The Red Shoes," "The Little Mermaid" is a more modern tale, first published in 1837. It was written as a kind of composite of siren fables and nymph myths, and is even darker than one might suppose from the more commonly seen, simplified retellings—even when one considers the versions where the little mermaid fails to win the heart of the prince at the end and is turned into sea-foam.

In Andersen's original story, the little mermaid is not merely motivated by love. She learns that because she is a mermaid, she has no soul, and therefore an eternity of nothingness awaits her after her death; the sea witch explains that the only way for her to "live forever" is to come into possession of an immortal soul, and the only way for this to happen is if she can get a human man to love her.

The little mermaid's desire for a soul—to avoid obliteration and endless darkness after her death—is twinned with, and just as strong if not stronger than, whatever desire she may feel for the prince. The witch warns the little mermaid that if she doesn't win the love of the prince, she won't get an immortal soul, because it is only through marriage and a pledge of faithfulness for all eternity that the prince's own soul can flow into her body and she can know the happiness of humans.

In order for her to attempt to achieve this, the witch must first take away nearly everything that makes the little mermaid herself. Although she has the loveliest voice of anyone at the bottom of the sea, she must win the prince's heart in silence. And although her tail will split into charming human legs, every step she takes will feel as if she were treading on pointed awls and sharp knives. The pain, however, stays hidden: *Hand in hand with her prince, she moved as lightly as a bubble, and he and everyone else marveled at her graceful gliding walk.*

Unlike in the Disney version, Andersen's little mermaid fails. The prince does not love her. On the morning after he marries another, when her life begins to leave her—her body turning to sea-foam—she is redeemed at the last minute by spirits of the air, who bring her to live as a star in the sky, like a nymph from Ovid. Like Karen in "The Red Shoes," she is only redeemed in death.

100

In fairy tales, women and girls are often asked to pay a price of pain, or silence, or both. In tales like "Bluebeard" and "Beauty and the Beast," daughters are things to give and barter, and their lives are left to the whims of tyrannical men who often later become their husbands. In "The Wild Swans," the protagonist, Elsa, must also remain silent while sewing shirts out of nettles to save her enchanted brothers, and cannot speak up even to defend herself when accused of witchcraft. In the end, she marries the king who nearly allowed her to be burned as a witch. The fairy tale marriage is about more than just the marriage itself: It is about salvation. It is, if you'll forgive me, a wife or death situation. With their silence and their suffering as payment, women and girls are obliged to buy their freedom, or the safety of their family, or their life, or love, or a soul. The silence and the pain are related.

101

In her book *The Body in Pain*, Elaine Scarry explains that one of the primary functions of pain is as a destroyer of language. Physical pain of all kinds defies meaningful description in its aftermath, and while it is happening, in extremis, it functions to dismantle speech into the kind of pre-linguistic sounds that can scarcely be deemed voluntary. As Virginia Woolf once wrote, *let a sufferer try to describe a pain in his head to a doctor and language at once runs dry.*

As if pain itself did not render one inarticulate enough, women have long been encouraged not only to tolerate physical pain, but to do so without complaining. Original sin lies conveniently with Eve, a woman wanting knowledge. Expelled from Eden, she pays for her knowledge with pain, like the little mermaid. In the Disney retelling of Andersen's maritime tale, the price of pain is eclipsed by silence, to soften it for younger, contemporary audiences. *It won't cost much, just your voice!* sings the octopod sea witch.

102

Bound feet have long since been left in the proverbial dustbin of history, but women are still expected to suffer for beauty. Modernity favors the self-oppressing woman. Women's pain (like our sexuality) is for spectacle, for public comment. It's not personal or private, but emblematic and therefore—unless it is somehow beautiful—it is tedious or shameful. Female pain is perhaps so ubiquitous as to be invisible, part of the architecture of both male and female lives, and upholding it depends on our silence.

Physical suffering is a fact of life that women are expected to assimilate in a way that men are not. It is perhaps because of this that women's pain is generally taken less seriously, even in a medical context. Reports have shown that women are in fact more biologically sensitive to pain than men. We feel it more, and yet when we report pain to doctors, it is statistically far more likely to be dismissed as psychological, or as an overreaction. We are less likely to be given pain medicine than men are and are more likely to be given sedatives. Another fairy tale solution, from "Sleeping Beauty" and "Briar Rose": when thorns surround you, just go to sleep.

103

It is a well-known maxim that women must suffer to be beautiful. It is a mantra we repeat to ourselves as we are tweezed, waxed, and threaded; as we endure another hour of cardio, or ignore pangs of hunger; as runway models swallow tissues and cotton balls in lieu of food to stay skeletal and employable; as we shiver in the cold while our dates stand secure in sturdy jeans and wool blazers; as the high heels that we have tolerated throughout an evening of dancing grow bolder and begin to make their assault at the end of the night, with ten blocks left to walk home.

The near universal acceptance of high heels says something about compulsory female handicap. Much of being a woman entails a kind of mass "consensual martyrdom," as coined by Brooklyn Museum director Lisa Small in a write-up of her exhibit *Killer Heels*. Perhaps women, like Eve, are taught that they deserve pain. This is true for more significant hurts, but also for quotidian pain. Forgotten pain. The kind of pain that we forget, that men are not asked to forget and would not forget. We come to confuse *tolerable* with comfortable and continue to move the line further and further as to what we are willing to tolerate. As Mary Karr wrote, *every pair of excruciating heels also telegraphs a subtle masochism*: that is, *I am a woman who can not only take an ass-whipping; to draw your gaze, I'll inflict one on myself.*

We can tell ourselves to be thankful, that it could be worse; that our toes could have been repeatedly broken and bound from the age of six; that we could be obligated to wear tight-laced corsets or painful girdles. But what if it is actually more than that? What if, rather than that we must suffer to be beautiful, what if it is actually true, at least on some level, that in order to be beautiful, we must suffer? Sweetness does not exist outside of the longing for sweetness. Our common understanding of it is backward: Sweetness was born with our evolutionary wiring to seek it out, because of what it did for us, and not the other way around. What if we, as a patriarchal society, have decided to find beautiful in women that which *causes* suffering? What if the suffering is actually the point?

104

In *The Bell Jar*, Plath's avatar, Esther, is plagued by the pain of a perpetual, airless, forced interiority. Beyond the now-familiar notion of a clinically depressed person being stuck inside their own head, forever retracing the same circle-scratching thoughts, the specific visual that Plath conjures is that of an inescapable enclosure—a bell jar—that follows her everywhere. The bell jar is a device for observable containment. She is trapped within the limits of her feminized, mid-century life, and inside her shiny, bloodied indoor shoes. The thing under the glass is not only kept separate; it is watched. (*There is terror in the public gaze.*) She can see the outside world, but her full involvement in it is an illusion, a false passage in the labyrinth. Where she thinks she sees a way forward, there is really a wall. Even when she is outside, she is really inside. There is an inside that she takes with her wherever she goes.

When Esther finally feels the bell jar of her depression lift, it is described as a collision with the outside world: *I felt my lungs inflate with the onrush of scenery—air, mountains, trees, people. I thought, "This is what it is to be happy."*

The character Esther Greenwood survives the book *The Bell Jar*, but Plath did not survive for even a month past its publication. She had described the quality of her despair as a pair of talons, clutching her heart. The young woman who wanted to travel west, to walk freely at night, ended up dying in a sealed kitchen at the age of thirty. In what may have been her very last poem, "Edge," composed just a few days before her death, she wrote:

Her bare
Feet seem to be saying:
We have come so far, it is over.

4 THE MINOTAUR

"I felt that the world was a labyrinth, from which it was impossible to flee . . ."
—JORGE LUIS BORGES, *DEATH AND THE COMPASS*

105

James Lloyd was a respected businessman, husband, and father of two. He owned a printing firm in Yorkshire, England. He was white, with a pleasant-enough face, piercing blue eyes, and a shock of salt-and-pepper hair that was more pepper than salt. One Saturday night in February of 1983, when he was still a young man, Lloyd went out to hunt for women in high heels as they walked home alone in the early hours of the morning after a night out on the town with friends. When he spotted one he found suitable, for whatever reason—because of her particular high heels, or because she was isolated enough, or unaware enough, or simply because she was there, and he felt it was finally time—he pulled a sheer stocking over his face to conceal his identity, grabbed her, and dragged her to a secluded spot on the grass.

When the attack was over—an attempted rape this time, assault without penetration—he fled the scene with her high-heeled shoes as trophy. Later that year he tried this again with another woman, also wearing high heels, and in a similar situation—a late night, an empty street, maybe a clumsiness in her step to suggest that drink had been taken—and this time, at knifepoint, he was successful. Once again, he took her shoes. Then he did it again. And again. At least six women in the area made reports to the police about a man who had raped them or attempted to rape them, and then stole their high heels. The youngest woman was eighteen and the oldest was fifty-four. The more crimes he committed, the more violent he got.

Here was a rapist in the classic, stereotypical mold: a stranger in the dark, a serial offender, in a public place, masking his face, using a weapon, with a likely fetish, preying on "respectable" women who were nevertheless dressed a certain way. Even so, the authorities could not catch him, and after a few years, in 1986, the trail of the Rotherham Shoe Rapist went cold.

106

Chrissie Hynde, the Rock and Roll Hall of Famer and lead singer of The Pretenders, was raped by a motorcycle gang when she was a young woman in Ohio. While doing press for her memoir, *Reckless*, in 2015, she told a journalist at the British *Sunday Times* that the attack was entirely her own fault. She did not blame the gang for raping her, but rather "took full responsibility." On the topic of rape in society more broadly, Hynde told her interviewer, *You know, if you don't want to entice a rapist, don't wear high heels so you can't run from him. . . . If you're wearing something that says "Come and fuck me," you'd better be good on your feet.*

Dance she did, and dance she must, right out into the dark forest.

107

And so, at the center of this maze, we find the Minotaur, that beast who haunts the corridors of our feminine labyrinth. Part man, part monster. He is here, in the shadows, waiting for us when we take a wrong turn. *Having met so many predators,* Rebecca Solnit writes, *I learned to think like prey.* Here then is the downside of the "choice" narrative, of what lies on the other side of wrong choices, or rather, the illusion of choice in an unequal world. Just as female empowerment is lately seen as a thing one can *choose,* (or, more often, buy)—individual, personal, internally harvested and externally displayed—so too is victimhood. It is the lie that you can control everything that happens to you, like items selected in a supermarket. Being *a victim* suddenly becomes not the simple fact of whether or not one has been acted upon by a perpetrator—

of sexual assault, of violence, of abuse—but rather, a state of mind and a statement of self. *I am not a victim*, says the raped woman who wants to show that she has agency, and choice, and hope, and most of all, the right attitude, because *victim* has become a pejorative. This, too, is a weapon in the Minotaur's hand. Agile, it can be turned this way and that; a benign thing, like a stone, which he can suddenly use to bludgeon you. Go where you want, dress how you want, but never forget how quickly the light of propriety can change. So says the Minotaur. The wrong-choosing woman is devoured.

108

In her book *The Purity Myth*, Jessica Valenti writes, *Now, should we treat women as independent agents, responsible for themselves? Of course. But being responsible has nothing to do with being raped. Women don't get raped because they weren't careful enough. Women get raped because someone raped them.*

109

Photographer Ruth Orkin's most famous photograph, *American Girl in Italy*, depicts a young painter named Jinx Allen at the age of twenty-three. She is walking down a street in Florence looking uncomfortable, while a group of men, old and young, leer and call to her with extravagant gusto. Originally published in *Cosmopolitan* in 1952, it became an iconic image that can be found in dorm rooms and pizza restaurants all over the world.

Orkin and Allen were both young, single, American women in creative professions traveling alone, who met at their hotel in Florence and became friends. Orkin, then thirty, decided to photograph Allen as she moved through the city, reenacting experiences both women had had while traveling alone—playfully looking at statues, asking police for directions, flirting with men in cafés, and yes, being harassed by strangers on the street.

The photo is a little bit staged. While the reactions and facial expressions of the men in the photo are authentic, Allen's expression of discomfort is feigned—or so she later claimed, at least in this instance. Allen said that she didn't mind the attention she received while traveling. But something—instinct? Other less savory experiences? The older Orkin?—compelled her to play out fear.

110

A woman is always seen to be *saying* something with her clothes, in ways that a man is not. It is as if, when a man speaks to a strange woman on the street, it is her skirt or her shoes that actually started the conversation. High heels are so ubiquitous in the upscale professional uniform for women, as well as in formal wear, as to be nearly compulsory in many places in the world. And yet the same shoes that were perfectly respectable in the boardroom or at the gala are suddenly read as a marker of sexual promiscuity when viewed on the same woman when she's walking home. (*If you're wearing something that says "Come and fuck me," you'd better be good on your feet.*)

There are "fuck-me pumps" and "fuck-me clothes," and, presumably, clothes and shoes that make no such demands, but there is little agreement as to what constitutes what. *The statements made by women's clothing are continually, willfully misread*, writes Naomi Wolf in *The Beauty Myth*. This is strange and dangerous territory, with different styles of cloth and leather interpreted as language. We engage in a "she said, it said" duality between a woman and her clothes. Shoes, read as an invitation, or even a command. *Fuck-me* pumps. A phrase in the imperative. But this sartorial phraseology is not universal and has different meaning in different settings. What says *appropriate* and *respectful* at the dinner party can be read as *whore* in the street, or later in the courtroom. It doesn't, really, but that is what the Minotaur will tell you.

111

The term *sexual harassment* was first coined in the 1970s and wasn't used in the legal system in America until the 1980s. The term *rape culture* was not coined until 2012. It means an environment where sexual violence is common, and a culture that instills in men a feeling of entitlement to women's bodies. Most women are taught to fear rape in ways that dramatically alter her movements, behavior, clothing, and freedom. In general, while men are also sometimes the victims of rape, they do not have this same experience.

112

One must be careful not to hold up the metaphor for the thing above the thing itself. Constrictive clothing and high heels might have prevented many Victorian women from climbing mountains, literal or figurative (although some did it anyway), but their problem was not one of fashion. What confines, impoverishes, exploits, enslaves, oppresses, sickens, bloodies, rapes, and kills women are not generally clothes or shoes, but rather laws and societal norms. Prejudice. Misogyny. White supremacy. Transphobia. Homophobia. Predatory corporations and unfair labor laws. Discriminatory work and hiring policies. Lack of legal protection from violence in the workplace, home, and street. Non-enforcement of existing protections. Weaponized bureaucracy. Overpriced women-specific services. Medical sexism. Religious sexism. Barred access to property ownership, financial management, a credit card, or a checkbook. Threat of violence in public spaces, both physical and virtual, and on public transportation systems. The mobility of women is and has been restricted physically through fashion, but most of all it has been restricted legally, financially, professionally, medically, intellectually, sexually, politically. That is to say, systemically.

113

In the Massachusetts colony in the seventeenth century, the arrival of the bewitching new high-heeled shoe styles from France led colony leaders to proclaim a law that "all women, whether virgins, maidens or widows" who used high-heeled shoes to seduce a man into marriage would be tried and punished as a witch. At that time, suspected witches in the colony were imprisoned, interrogated, publicly stripped, and tortured. Convicted witches were hanged. (The women of the Massachusetts colony left high heels alone.) In England in the late eighteenth century, a very similar law was proposed to the British parliament, by which women who wore high heels or used other cosmetic artifices like perfume, wigs, or false teeth to snare a husband, would face the same penalties as witches, and the marriage would be considered null and void. The British law didn't pass, but the sentiment was out there.

114

In 2008, in Kota Baru, a city in northern Malaysia, the conservative municipal council distributed pamphlets indicating that female workers should abstain from wearing lipstick and high heels, so as to "preserve their dignity" and to avoid "incidents like rape and illicit sex." In modern times, high heels and other women's fashions are less often labeled as actual witchcraft, but are frequently blamed for rape and harassment, as if shoes cast a spell that a perpetrator can't resist.

115

Most people who see Ruth Orkin's famous Italian photo don't know the woman is named Jinx, or that she's a painter, or that she's 6 feet tall in flat shoes, or that she's only pretending to be afraid. In a way, the woman in the photo *isn't* Jinx, she's just a woman, and she isn't in danger from these men. When it ran in *Cosmo*, the caption read: *Public admiration . . . shouldn't fluster you. Ogling the ladies is a popular, harmless and flattering pastime you'll run into in many foreign countries. The gentlemen are usually louder and more demonstrative than American men, but they mean no harm.*

An interview with Allen further served to reassure audiences that she was in on the game: *Oh, and that poor soul touching himself? I was used to it. It was almost like a good luck sign for the Italian man, making sure the family jewels were intact. When it was first published, that was occasionally airbrushed out but I would never consider it to be a vulgar gesture. . . . My expression is not one of distress, that was just how I stalked around the city. I saw myself as Beatrice of Dante's Divine Comedy. You had to walk with complete assurance and maintain a dignity at all times. The last thing you would do would be to look them in the eye and smile. I did not want to encourage them. This image has been interpreted in a sinister way but it was quite the opposite. They were having fun and so was I.*

Jinx Allen, cool girl. For her, none of these men whistling and jeering and grabbing their junk had turned violent. Their questions to her were not sincere. She knew, however, that she could not look them in the eye. She was very young, and uncommonly tall, and quite beautiful. She was not wearing high heels. The city was full of men with nothing to do in the late morning, because it was just after the war, and work was scarce. She was fortunate that they did not truly ask anything of her. What they wanted, and what most men calling to women from street corners want, is to express their own masculinity against the fleeting image of the passing woman. They are exerting their right to their masculinity, and to public space. The woman herself does not matter most of the time, and in a way is not even real to them.

116

Photographer Katherine Cambareri was disturbed by the prevalence of victim-blaming in incidents of sexual assault. Hoping to counteract the narrative that "her high heels were asking for it," she decided to produce a series of photographs of the clothes real women were wearing when attacked. The images are startling in their mundanity. The items appear slightly crumpled against a dark background. Baggy track pants. T-shirts that look like they came from Old Navy, both short- and long-sleeved. A pair of dangling Converse sneakers. A pair of Anne Taylor Loft blue jeans. A short black dress with a flared skirt. A plaid flannel shirt. A loose red cardigan. A black tank top with pink roses on it. Emptied of the woman herself, the idea of blaming these inanimate objects for rape is even more absurd. We were never blaming the clothes, or even the choice to wear them. We were always blaming the woman.

117

Who is the Minotaur? He is a metaphor but so, in many ways, is the high heel. A woman in heels can't get far, or not for long. We are told, again and again, that every woman walks through the world with the anatomical equivalent of an expensive watch, or a wallet packed with cash, and that she should be careful about where she displays this equivalent thing, or else it might get stolen. As if rape were like a mugging.

But what is this "thing" that a woman should not flaunt, the way a man should not walk down the street with a fistful of hundreds? Is it her beauty? Her legs? Her cleavage? Her toes showing through her shoes? Her face? Her butt in tight jeans?

The way her butt sticks out more when she wears high heels? What if she has a butt that sticks out like that anyway? Should she not leave the house? Should a woman only wear long, loose dresses and flats, like the Amish, and if this still "entices a rapist," should she wear a headscarf? And if this is not enough, an abaya, or a niqab? What if she is raped anyway? Is it because she was outside without a man? Should women not go outside, or not go outside alone? What about the nuns who are raped, the grandmothers, and the little girls in footie pajamas? What did they do to entice their rapists? Are there two kinds of rapists, the kind that must be enticed, and the kind that doesn't need enticement? Considering the broad range of women and girls who are raped, in a broad range of outfits and situations, how does one know what a particular rapist finds "enticing?" Why must we accept the omnipresent violence of men against women, like it is the weather, and then treat women like witches who have conjured the weather? If she was wearing high heels, and floats when we throw her in the river, then she's a witch and must have enticed her rapist. We're not saying it's *all* her fault, but what did she expect? In "The Wild Swans," Hans Christian Andersen writes, *Out of the city streamed the entire populace; they wanted to see the witch burn.*

Like the women's fashion guides that (still) tell women how to dress to be deserving of respect in a business setting, in a world that routinely disrespects them for reasons having nothing to do with their clothes, so, too, are women told *ad nauseum* how to dress in order to avoid rape. Very high heels are associated in particular with two castes of women: the social elite, and the sex worker. But who gets to decided who is who, and in which circumstances? Perhaps raped women in "provocative" clothing and shoes aren't just "asking for it," but are, like Karen in "The Red Shoes," seen as being punished for an attempt to rise above their station. If you can't be one—an elite woman—then you must be the other—a prostitute, who is seen not as a businesswoman with wares to sell, but as public property, the money that passes hands a mere technicality. Most women are neither, but society can decide, sometimes on a whim, where it thinks you really belong.

In trying to explain why women's clothing and footwear is partially or entirely to blame for rape, the armchair devil's advocate routinely compares the sexy woman to a man who fails to protect his property. But this reduces women to property, and our sexuality to a public or private resource that must be guarded, or else is free for the taking. As if our attractiveness—this thing that culture aggressively compels us to pursue at all times, and at all points in our lives in order to have worth as women—is suddenly a terrible and dangerous mistake. Usually, when a victim is questioned about her outfit or behavior in cases of harassment or rape, the concern is not so much about the details of these things, but about ascertaining *what kind of woman* she is; it falls back on the age-old caste system for women, with private "good" women who belong to one man, and are therefore off limits, and public "bad" women who belong to everyone. In Jon Krakauer's book *Missoula: Rape and the Justice System in a College Town*, girls who've been assaulted are asked by police afterward if they have a boyfriend. There is no right answer. Not having one means that you were fair game, but having one means that you probably just cheated and are now reporting rape so as not to be caught, or out of regret for your transgression against the man who has a right to you, by having sex with a man who does not. But rape is not about sex. Rapists do not rape because they want sex. They rape because they want to rape. It is not about high heels or beauty or the lack of it, guarded or unguarded. It is, of course, about power.

118

James Lloyd, the Rotherham Shoe Rapist, was not caught for nearly twenty years; during that time he married, started a family, and took a second job as a taxi driver, which meant that he was often out alone, roaming the town, until very late at night. When his identity was finally discovered by police, in an operation led by Detective Inspector Angela Wright, they wondered if they might find the six pairs of high heels that he had taken as trophies from the women who reported him to the authorities. When police raided his office at the printing firm, they did find six pairs of high heels—as well as an additional one hundred and twenty.

These were not fetish shoes, and they were not new. They were high heels that a woman might wear to work in the morning if she worked in an office, or out to a nice restaurant or music venue on a Saturday night. Most were black, with some red, white, burgundy, silver, blue, and turquoise. They were worn. Walked in. There were so many. Police photos show the enormous stash laid out on a table the way one might normally see weapons or piles of cash seized from a drug cartel. Detective Inspector Wright told media that she now believed the true number of Lloyd's victims "could be much higher."

119

Even by the most conservative estimates, only a small portion of rapes are ever reported to the police. Going by the statistics that the Rape, Abuse & Incest National Network (RAINN) uses, about two out of every three rapes in the United States, or some 66 percent, go entirely unreported to authorities. But according to the American Centers for Disease Control and Prevention's National Intimate Partner and Sexual Violence Survey, the number of reported rapes is less than 7 percent of the total rapes committed. Which means, of course, that 93 percent were not reported, let alone prosecuted or even investigated.

120

Jinx Allen, traveling alone through postwar Florence, said that she saw herself as Beatrice, one of Dante's guides through the realms of the dead in his *Divine Comedy*. Perhaps this is simply because Beatrice was a Florentine, and beautiful like

Jinx, but for me it brings to mind other associations. When Dante reaches the seventh circle of hell, which is reserved for those souls damned for their natures, he meets the Minotaur, their captain and jailer. With the body of a man and the head of a bull, he presides over the zone of violence in Dante's hell and represents the bestial violence of men.

The original story of the Minotaur goes like this: The wife of King Minos of Crete, Pasiphäe, hides within a wooden cow to have sex with a bull, and produces a monstrous offspring. To hide this shame, Minos shuts the Minotaur up inside the labyrinth and sends in youths and maidens at regular intervals to be his sacrifice, before he is eventually slayed by Theseus with the help of Ariadne and her ball of twine. The Minotaur embodies the urges of man, but without man's civilized intellect. A poisoned masculinity. For sustenance, he devours both men and women. Lacking a human mind, he is unaware, does not know he is a monster, and even hurts himself.

121

Ted Hughes's last publication before his death in 1998 was his translation, from the French, of Racine's play *Phèdre*. In it, the eponymous heroine invokes the Minotaur and his labyrinth in a famous passage. This speech was of particular importance to Hughes, and echoed aspects of his own writing, notably *Birthday Letters*, his collections of poems about his first wife, Sylvia Plath.

In his earlier poem "The Bull Moses," Hughes employs the image of a bull in dark confinement to visualize the depth and intricacy of mental space. In the *Birthday Letters* poem "Your Paris," about his and Plath's honeymoon, Hughes imagines the City of Light as his new wife's mental labyrinth, in which she roamed, herself Minotaur-like in her black high heels, hunting for the monster-father-lover for whom she thirsted:

> *a labyrinth*
> *Where you still hurtled, scattering tears*
> *Was a dream where you could not*
> *Wake or find the exit or*
> *The Minotaur to put a blessed end*
> *To the torment.*

Another poem from that collection, called "The Minotaur," opens with his wife's frustrations that her duties as a wife and mother did not leave her enough time to write, and the furniture-breaking rage that ensued. To Hughes, the monster in Plath's maze was the mythologized specter of her father, *horned and bellowing*, but also, ultimately, herself.

122

In Jorge Luis Borges's story about the Minotaur in his book *Labyrinths*, the beast is childlike in his lack of awareness.

Yet his obliviousness is yet another tool in the arsenal of his violence, and he goes on devouring youths and maidens just the same. To him, all of this is normal. He describes his labyrinth as "a house."

The house is the same size as the world; or rather, it is the world, Borges's Minotaur says.

123

The dominant narratives in society and media still struggle to see women as individuals. We are more often flavors, types. Public feminist intellectuals are routinely castigated for criticizing individual women with whom they disagree, even when that disagreement has not been expressed in a gendered or sexist manner. This comes up a lot when women fight about whether or not they should wear high heels. When women are not seen fully as people, we are all the same, and criticizing one of us means criticizing all of us. Concepts of a female individuality that includes flaws, adversaries, and even villains, is denied.

Even now, as a woman, to be flawed in any way is to be deserving of erasure—that is, she, too, deserves to be devoured. As culture critic Jia Tolentino writes: *It's the same with feminism as it is with women in general: there are always, seemingly, infinite ways to fail.*

124

Ours is a world that devours women regularly, and not just with sexual violence. We subsume them in workplaces where the decks are stacked against them. We bury them under domestic tasks. We barrage them with demands on their time and finances to strive to be ever more beautiful. We leave their stories disproportionately untold. They disappear from their own lives suddenly and we do not send our voices up in outcry, because their skin was the wrong (darker) color.

Betty Friedan's *The Feminine Mystique* is often dismissed now as a period piece, out of touch with the realities of modern women. But her cherry bomb of a book, thrown into the sitting rooms of white mid-century suburbia, was explicitly for and about housewives like her. It didn't claim to be about the women at the time who *did* work, either through brilliance and force of will in esteemed, male-dominated careers, or through necessity in the backbreaking ranks of the working class, for whom boredom and intellectual stagnation may have seemed like luxuries. Rather, she chillingly chronicles a kind of metastasizing, malignant, commodified femininity, the exaggerated gender binary used as weapon to subdue a generation of women, pressgang them into lifelong wageless labor, and turn even the most privileged among them into a servant class.

Although Friedan did not explicitly make this observation herself, every woman, regardless of race, social status, or ability, was and is a member of that subordinate social class of women. This expectation, that women should live for, cater to, defer to, and define themselves always in relationship to approval from men, was and is far from a white-middle-class-only problem.

Friedan, formerly a labor journalist before becoming a housewife, later described herself as writing from within her own captivity inside the feminine mystique, and its pages bear the distortions of that vantage point. But nowhere did Friedan claim that women did not exist who broke the mold, or whose reduced societal position made the mold aspirational at best, or impossible. Rather, Friedan's target was the mold itself—that thing that American media was urging women to strive for was dangerous and wrong. She was not against femininity, but rather the ways in which patriarchal culture twisted the definition of femininity so as to remove women from public space and public participation.

Where Friedan's book failed and opened her work up to later be dismissed by some in its entirety, was in her entrenched homophobia, the absence of intersectionality, her embrace of now-outdated psychoanalytic and pseudo-scientific nonsense regarding the effect of a woman's attitude and character on her family and body, and a lack of accountability ascribed to individual men. However, where it is lastingly successful, *The Feminine Mystique* showed that even the supposed ultimate prize of white, affluent mid-century American womanhood was in fact an oppressive lie. She recognized that to free women from the bonds of their servitude, structural societal change was necessary. In the earlier pages of the book, Friedan documented, in a scholarly manner, a very real and quite disturbing historical revisionism; a rolling back of cultural support for the personal and professional gains made by women in the 1920s, 1930s, and 1940s, which, of course, did not simply occur of their own volition, but were fought for, tooth and nail, by women thinkers, writers, workers, and activists of all backgrounds, from at least as far back as the eighteenth century.

125

What we are seeing now, with the #MeToo Movement, is a glimpse at the extent to which women are still expected or compelled to submit to men, either through sexual bullying in professional settings, or through a persistent culture of intimidation, fear, and obligation that exists in women's personal relationships with men. Young women are speaking up, now perhaps more than ever before, not just about the sexual interactions they are forced to have against their will, but about the sex they ostensibly consent to but that they do not want and do not enjoy, but which they decide to endure anyway. They do this because they fear hurting a man's feelings, not meeting expectations, or, more likely, fear the hostility, wrath, and possibly even violence that commonly results from doing so. The terms of our service agreement may have changed since the days of *The Feminine Mystique*, but service is still expected.

126

In "slut walks," a performance-based style of protest against rape culture commonly seen on college campuses, women march while dressed in sexy or revealing clothing, lingerie, and high heels, often with the slogan STILL NOT ASKING FOR IT painted on signs and on their bodies. In another performative protest model, men don high heels and other traditionally feminine accessories in order to "walk a mile in her shoes," to raise awareness for victims of sexual harassment and assault. Of course, *her shoes* are high heels.

127

Is there something inherently sexual about high heels? Freud, gesturing wildly at the phallic shaft of the heel itself, would tell you an emphatic *yes*. Fetish shoes are almost always high heels, no matter what is currently popular in the mainstream.

In Paris, I found myself in the archives of the prefecture of police, looking through arrest records from the nineteenth century. There were entire, enormous, ornate books devoted to pornographic photography and the people who were making it, as well as the women who were forced to register as prostitutes or cross-dressers. (The author George Sand, herself known to cross-dress on the streets of mid-nineteenth-century Paris, did so illegally, without registering.)

We're used to seeing the almost quaint, shy nudes of Victorian erotic pictures, but there was nothing demure about this French stuff. This was hardcore, and I imagined the poor models having to hold these poses for the extra-long duration of the primitive exposure, trying to look like they were in the throes of passion. Unlike the nude nymphs and goddesses so common in sculpture and paintings of that time, these women of the Second Empire's pornography were always wearing high-heeled shoes. It marked them as *naked*, rather than simply nude; as women without clothes on, rather than nymphs or goddesses. High heels have been an important part of pornography ever since.

128

Nowhere else in society is the subjectivity of attraction so nakedly displayed than in cases of harassment and assault, with both ends of the beauty spectrum used to dismiss any complaint. In rape culture, rape is simultaneously the gravest threat, a catchall corrective, and a thing that a woman must meet some imaginary standard to be worthy of. A woman's accusation can be dismissed with the idea that she "asked for it" by dressing too sexy, or, conversely, she can be dismissed as not attractive enough to be harassed or assaulted, as President Trump did with his alleged victims while on the campaign trail in 2016. As if either were a compliment.

"Well, if you say you haven't, you're a prude. If you say you have, you're a slut," warns Ally Sheedy's character in the 1985 film *The Breakfast Club*. "It's a trap."

Today on the Indian subcontinent, the commonly used term for public sexual harassment is "Eve teasing." This implies that the victim, like the original woman Eve, is not so much being harassed, but *tempted*, as by the serpent, into a state of sin due to her weaker, carnal nature. By this logic, of course, it may have been naughty of the men to lure her away from her Edenic purity, with their grabbing hands, their coarse language and their catcalls, but in the end the choice to engage was probably hers.

In 1999, it became enshrined in Italian case law that it was not possible for a man to rape a woman if she was wearing tight jeans. If she was wearing tight jeans, the argument went, it wasn't rape, because it's too hard to take tight jeans off, and therefore the woman must have helped the man to get into her pants, signaling consent. The ruling was not overturned until nearly a decade later, in 2008, when a man was accused of sexually assaulting his partner's sixteen-year-old daughter by shoving his hands into her jeans. He tried to argue that the jeans were tight, and so he could not have committed the acts against her will. The court did not accept his defense, however, and ruled that "jeans cannot be compared to any type of chastity belt."

129

Within the last decade, the United States has instituted a new legal definition of rape. Before 2011 that definition was much more archaic: *the carnal knowledge of a female, forcibly and against her will.* Now, it is defined as *the penetration, no matter how slight, of the vagina or anus with any body part or object, or oral penetration by a sex organ of another person, without the consent of the victim.* Importantly, this new definition not only acknowledged male and non-binary victims of rape for the first time by removing "female" from the requirement, but it also introduced a new concept, whose absence indicated that a rape had occurred: consent. Formerly, unless a woman was physically overpowered—*forcibly*—a rape had not taken place. But there are issues with both definitions, since what counts as "force" and what gets construed as "consent" are, like the statements made by women's clothes, routinely misinterpreted.

Many people still seem to struggle with the fact that saying yes to a date isn't the same thing as agreeing to make out. Just like wanting to make out isn't the same thing as wanting to have sex. And wanting to have a certain kind of sex one time doesn't mean you are consenting to whatever sexual act, at whatever time, for however long, that the other person can think of. As in Italy with tight jeans, these imaginary, nonverbal indicators of consent are often stretched to include what the victim is wearing.

Most stranger rapes do not happen on a whim. The Rotherham Shoe Rapist—exactly the kind of monster that women are supposed to avoid by "not dressing sexy"—wasn't suddenly overcome with violent desire upon seeing a woman in high heels. He planned, brought supplies, and shaped his life around his attacks. He was a predator with a particular fixation. The shoes were not the point.

130

In early 2016, a married PhD student named Eva Hagberg Fisher dressed in jeans, a silky top from the Gap, and a jacket, in order to deliver an 11-page account of sexual harassment by her former graduate school adviser at the University of California at Berkeley. *I wanted to look good*, Fisher later wrote, *I also wanted to look credible.*

In her essay in the *New York Times* about dressing for "the full-time job that is being an objector to sexual harassment in America," she shares the agonizingly specific target she had to aim at of respectability, credibility, strength, and "just plausibly sexy enough to look like you could have been harassed but 100 percent wasn't asking for it." During the hearing process, she was subjected to intrusive, irrelevant questions and accusations about her personal life, including about the age of a previous partner (older than her), and how quickly she slept with her now-husband—things that, of course, have nothing to do with whether or not she was sexually harassed. But those involved with the hearings, like rape trial prosecutors and juries the world over, were looking to determine less what happened to her and more *what kind of woman* she was. Which is why, she had intuited, her clothes were so important.

At the beginning of what she knew would be a difficult semester due to the sexual harassment complaint, Fisher bought herself a pair of black high-heeled Alexander Wang ankle booties with hints of rose gold. The heels were thick and sturdy, more like the shoes that Louis XIV would wear, minus the red silk, than like the stilettos that Roger Vivier marketed to 1950s women in thrall to the feminine mystique. She thought of them as empowering. She called them her *Wonder Woman-inspired boots*, her *"I can do this" boots*. But she soon found she couldn't wear them. For that elusive, plausibly-sexy-but-not-asking-for-it, not-too-feminine, non-victim-identified, credible, respectful, professional-but-imp overished-grad-student, appropriate-for-a-legal-proceeding look, she found that loafers were the thing—also black turtlenecks, so as not to show any skin. And always wearing her hair up. And never being photographed at home or sitting down. She writes, *I wish that we lived in a world where I could both wear high-heeled gold-detailed boots and be utterly reliable and credible, but the patriarchy is still too strong. Talk about a narrow path to victory.*

131

There are situations in which certain choices are obligatory, writes Elena Ferrante in *The Story of a New Name*. In the novel, a woman tries to dream herself out of poverty and patriarchy, fairy-tale-like, by designing shoes—but fails. Not all choices are freely chosen. Some choices are made blind. In the best con jobs, the mark is manipulated into thinking that it was their own idea to do what the con artist wanted of them all along.

132

There are so many different ways to be devoured. Because of this, the Minotaur is not always who you think he will be. He can wear the mask of someone you have trusted. He can wear the mask of another woman. He does not discriminate. Maybe the Minotaur is you. Maybe, in my inevitable blindness, I have erred or wronged you through obliviousness or omission in this text. For example, I don't actually know if any of the Rotherham Shoe Rapist's victims had been drinking, I just made assumptions and threw in a "maybe."

Maybe I am the Minotaur, too.

133

Not too long after the horde of stolen high heels was carried down from James Lloyd's office in Yorkhire, he was convicted of six counts of rape and attempted rape. There was a DNA match to semen samples taken from his victims. In 2006, he was sentenced to spend at least fifteen years in prison, just over two years for each woman who reported their attack, despite the 120 additional pairs of high heels that may have belonged to other victims. However, after just seven years, the Court of Appeals reduced his sentence, and he was released in 2013.

134

The thing about a labyrinth is that, unlike mazes, there really isn't much choice involved at all. There are twists and turns, things to fool the eye and dampen the spirit, but there are no differing roads to choose from, no multiple passageways running off into the shadows. Strictly speaking, it is the maze that has forking paths. With labyrinths, which is where the Minotaur lives, all you must do is go on. The test of a labyrinth, then, is not one of intelligence or even luck, but of endurance, physical and psychological. And it has a unique lesson, too—one that you can only find by putting one foot in front of the other.

Sometimes when you think you are nearing the end, you are actually quite far from it, and find that, really, you're just starting out. Likewise, sometimes when all is darkest, and you think that all is lost, you are actually almost at the finish. Like Theseus, you take hold of Ariadne's thread. You must find strands to connect and guide you wherever you can. Is this a strange, dark time for women, or are we finally, only now, starting to come out into the light again, and in ways that we never have before? Perhaps we are finally showing the Minotaur for what he is, and in this way, he can finally be defeated. We're not quite there yet, but the only way is through.

5 A GODDESS AT THE END OF THE WORLD

*"I can't tell you how much
my boots delighted me . . .
with those steel-tipped heels I was
solid on the sidewalk at last."*

—GEORGE SAND

135

The woman in the black cocktail dress and stiletto high heels stands at the edge of a dazzling pool in the middle of the jungle. Once upon a time, hundreds of virgin girls were drowned here as sacrifice to the gods. A gravesite. Without taking off her dress or stilettos, the woman enters the clear water. Her taloned shoes sink down into the sand at the bottom, kicking up clouds. The light under the surface is hazy, golden. She isn't alone. A white stallion has plunged in after her. His hooves and her heels beat against the soft blue-green. He rushes past her and her body arcs back, her feet suspended, like a matador with the power of levitation. He swims, she swims, heels and hooves both out of their element. The beast is powerful, and dangerous in his own way, but no predator. It is the woman who is in pursuit. She catches him, and climbs onto his back. The dark spikes of her heels press against his pale withers. It has become a kind of dance. Later, they stand side by side in the sand, with the spidery underwater light spangled over them, the shape of their muscular legs twinned, like equals.

This isn't a dream, or a fiction, but something that really happened. The place is a *cenote*, a sinkhole in Tulum, on Mexico's Yucatan peninsula. The year is 2012, and the woman is Mexican artist Ana Teresa Fernandez. She calls her work *social sculptures*, staged events that star a heroic, hyper-femme version of herself. It's a persona she has referred to as her *protagonist*. These social sculptures are then spun into short films, video installations, photographs, and photorealist paintings. Of her impulse to ride a white stallion in this *cenote*, a site of Mayan virgin sacrifice, she said she wondered, *How come boys get to come of age by conquering some part of nature, and women instead get killed in nature?*

The actions performed in Fernandez's paintings are both mundane and superhuman. Quotidian, and yet somehow outside time. Her protagonist is at once ordinary and

Olympian. She can be seen ironing her hair, scouring a bathtub, hanging laundry on a clothesline, or at the shoreline mopping up the sea, bringing the sky down to erase the US-Mexico border fence with blue paint—all while wearing a little black dress and black stiletto high heels. Her heroine's uniform. She has said that her work is about telling stories to erase the distance between the known and the unknown, to encourage empathy with that which is hard to digest. She has expressed an interest in mythmaking, or re-making, and in rewriting fairy tales.

136

I began this book in Paris, but am finishing it very far from there. I went west, as Plath wanted to do, following the thread of things unavailable to women fifty years ago. Or at least, not like this. I'm writing this from El Paso, where I have traveled alone, and where I can see, across an international border, the looking-glass Mexican city of Ciudad Juárez, mirroring back America's dirty secrets. A rose-gold full moon has risen up into a horizon of violet smoke. I am here because the area's Immigration and Customs Enforcement detention centers are overflowing with men, women and children who are caught in a dark maze. They have been walking for months through jungle, mountain, and desert, fleeing violence in their home countries of Guatemala, Honduras, and El Salvador.

137

The image of a high heel, and a red high heel in particular, is like a hieroglyph meaning *woman*. If it's on a bathroom door in a restaurant, it means that men shouldn't go in—there's probably an equivalent door with a mustache or a cowboy boot nearby. Likewise, when a red high heel appears on the cover of a book, it usually indicates to men that they don't have to read it. That it's not for them. But the image can be used to garner empathy in other settings.

In photographs of piled shoes taken from victims of the Holocaust, the eye is drawn to the inevitable red high-heeled sandal, flung like a woman's body on that drab and terrible mountain, or churned partially under.

In Ciudad Juárez since the 1990s, hundreds of women have been murdered, and thousands more have disappeared, in what has been called "a femicide." Many of those whose bodies were discovered had been mutilated or sexually assaulted. Most cases remained unsolved, with officials blaming the women for their own deaths—the sexy high heels they were wearing, or the places they were walking. Telephone poles were covered with flyers bearing the faces of the missing. The rate of death and disappearance was so high, and the crimes so gruesome, that Juárez was nicknamed "the city that kills women." Since 2009, Mexican artist Elina Chauvet has sought to draw attention to these murders—and to murdered women everywhere—with a touring art installation. Called *Los Zapatos Rojos*, it consists of women's shoes—dozens to hundreds, depending on the setting—set up in pairs in a public square, all red, all used, many high heeled but some not, symbolizing the women who are no longer here to wear them.

138

I know a woman who pole dances recreationally, wearing the tall platform heels usually described as "stripper shoes." The exaggerated heel is for aesthetic purposes, but it is also functional, used to grip the pole. A longtime body positivity activist, she finds this kind of dance freeing. It's a way to claim her own athleticism and creativity—the creativity of externalized desire. It doesn't matter who is watching; often no one is. She does it for herself. If, as Margaret Atwood says, there is really a man inside her mind, watching, giving approval—how much does it matter if the end result is one of joy? Can we really pare away those parts of us bruised by culture, and still be whole?

A friend of mine teaches burlesque dancing and the art of the strip tease to shy women, using high heels and lingerie. When they finally grow more comfortable expressing themselves, her students often shed tears of release as something frozen inside of them melts away. It is an emotional experience to get in touch with these deep aspects of themselves—pride, playfulness, sexuality—that have previously been barred by fear or shame, and which the trappings of cultural femininity can help them liberate.

The son of another friend has adored dressing in "girl's" clothes since early childhood. In preschool he gravitated toward tiaras and princess frocks. Now, since his teen years, that interest has been elevated into a vocation as the campiest of drag queens. When it comes time for Pride parades, his straight parents march with him out of support, with mom, dad, and son all done up in exaggerated makeup, dresses, wigs, and heels.

A five-foot-tall woman in four-inch high heels has increased her physical stature by 6.6 percent—not quite the 8 percent size advantage that men have over women on average, but she is getting closer.

139

Ana Teresa Fernandez's images are dreamlike, magical, but every scene really happened. In one performance, she swaps her black stilettos for a pair of high heels made entirely from ice. She stands over a grate on a boulevard in West Oakland until they melt. In the art photos taken beforehand, they look like glass slippers, cruel and strange against her warm flesh. She called the work *Ice Queen*, but also *La Llorona*, after the weeping female ghost from Latin American folk tales. The ice shoes disintegrated tear by tear. She is referencing other folk tales here, too. *I wanted to melt away that age-old myth, of Cinderella, a woman behind closed doors, needing to be rescued,* she said. Her work has an air of defiance, or triumph. Her protagonist persona may be classically feminine, but she is always subject, never object, deftly slipping between fantasy and reality with the grace of a dancer.

In another piece called *Ablutions*, which Fernandez made as a response to being called a *mojada*, a wetback, she can be seen doing laps in a swimming pool, still in her dress and high heels, to wash the grime of that racial slur from her body. In a 2017 talk about her work, in Washington, DC, she referred to this unconventional swimming garb as *the drag of femininity*. It was not immediately clear if she meant that it was a form of drag, as in the costume of performed femaleness, or drag as in that which slows down a body in motion through water or air, holding it back.

140

It is hard to parse female objectification from female sensuality, that undiscovered country of femininity outside of male influence and control. But just as surely as high heels can and have been used to enforce rigid ideas of gender, so too can they be used to subvert them.

Men have dressed as women for millennia, for reasons ranging from art, spirituality, and personal expression, to derogatory minstrelsy. In Shakespeare's time, all professional actors were men, and so the original Juliet, Desdemona,

Viola, and Lady Macbeth were all played by men, too, with utmost seriousness. Since several of Shakespeare's most famous female characters themselves cross-dress in his plays, audiences saw men as women, and also men as women as men. By the nineteenth century, even though female actors were allowed on the stage, it was not uncommon for men to portray women for comedic effect. Drag can be deployed maliciously, to mock gay men and women, particularly women of color, as was done near the turn of the last century by white American men in drag and blackface. But more often, contemporary drag is a celebration of male-expressed femininity and unconventional gender identities. In many instances, drag has become its own look, a kind of hyperbolic womanhood. As RuPaul once said, *I do not impersonate females. How many women do you know who wear seven-inch heels, four-foot wigs, and skintight dresses?* And, *I don't dress like a woman; I dress like a drag queen.* This too is myth making.

Eddie Izzard, erstwhile self-styled executive transvestite, is part of yet another tribe, that of male-identified or non-binary individuals for whom wearing "women's" clothes is neither a performance nor an impersonation, but a part of who they are that feels right and natural. Recent paparazzi photos of Izzard in New York show him dressing almost exactly the way I do when I'm running around a city: jeans, a button-down shirt, high-heeled ankle boots, and a pop of bright lipstick.

141

For the past five hundred years, whenever excess has been celebrated in Western male fashion, some form of high-heeled shoe has been a part of it. Our notions of sartorial virility are as changing as our ideals of female beauty. For seventeenth-century Europeans, a high-heeled boot, a full-skirted frock coat, and a long mane of flowing hair were the height of manliness. Male ostentation went out of vogue after the French Revolution, but heeled shoes for men never really went away; they simply drew less attention to themselves. Men's custom-made shoes were produced with varying heel heights from one to three inches throughout the nineteenth century and after, depending on the needs and vanities of the client.

Then came the gender-bending 1970s, and suddenly all bets were off. Glam rock burst onto the music scene in a metallic-confetti collision of old Hollywood glamour, cabaret theatrics, and science fiction. Not since the vertiginous *chopines* of the Venetians had the Western world seen anything quite like the towering, glittering high-heeled platform shoes worn by this new species of male celebrity and their fans. Fashion historians have attributed the entry of 1970s men's platform heels into mainstream culture as coming from a few directions, namely the peacocking "pimp" fashions of Blaxploitation films, as well as the rise in visibility of sexual subcultures and gender-non-conforming artists and musicians. Preludes can also be seen in the Cuban-heeled Chelsea boots and winklepickers worn by the Beatles and the Rolling Stones a decade prior.

Suddenly, the male body was being presented for the female gaze in ways that it never had been before. Icons like David Bowie, Lou Reed, Alice Cooper, and Elton John all wore platform heels onstage and off. A disturbingly sexy Tim Curry appeared as the bisexual, genderqueer alien scientist Frank N. Furter in *The Rocky Horror Picture Show*, wearing rhinestone-studded platform cabaret heels made by iconic London glam rock shoe designer Terry de Havilland. Mostly, rather than feminizing these male stars, the shoes were perceived as dandyish, hypermasculine and conspicuously sexual.

But while platforms and raised heels did find their way onto some ordinary men's feet during the 1970s, it never became the standard daily style for men in business or other, less artistic professions, the way that high heels have long been for women. By the 1980s, the style had largely disappeared, although some male artists, like Prince and David Bowie, continued to wear toned-down versions. Fashion magazines and blogs will sometimes declare that heels for men are on their way back again. But despite the best efforts of bold designers and peacocking fashionistos, it hasn't happened yet.

142

Feeling powerful is not the same thing as being empowered, but they are not unrelated. Both have their merits. One of the key ways women have been oppressed in the last century has been through a relentless culture-wide onslaught against self-esteem, leaving them too preoccupied with the supposed unacceptability of their own bodies to work to improve the systems that affect their lives. Because of this, boosting a woman's confidence *can* help spur her to action, toward achieving good in her own life, but also toward social change. This is not to say that feeling pretty is a prerequisite for political involvement—not at all. But in a culture that shouts women down at nearly every turn, and equates beauty with female worth, it makes sense to take a personal boost of confidence wherever one can get it; to take control of one's sexuality and see oneself as a sexual subject rather than a sexual object; to celebrate different kinds of feminine beauty. To act. To choose. To be a protagonist.

143

While Ana Teresa Fernandez offers us the image of a woman in high heels in the jungle, Firelei Baez, painter of efflorescing female forms, gives us women who are jungles in high heels. Both artists are trying to invent a new kind of femininity outside patriarchy and white supremacy. Baez's paintings, with her women sprouting leaves, remind me of Daphne in Ovid—except that they have legs. They are women who've become trees that are mobile and can flower wherever they want. These changes of shape, these new forms, are where we recreate ourselves. *A man tries to dream another man into existence*, Borges writes. *In the end he realizes that he has been dreamed into existence by another.*

144

What must we put women through in order to allow them to be viewed as protagonists? In movies of the twenty-first century, only about one-quarter to one-third in any given year have had women as main characters. Of that already small percentage, less than a third were older than 40, and even fewer were women of color. Fewer still were those who do not fit current beauty ideals. Our lives are still saturated by fairy tales and mythmaking: the myth of female inferiority, and the fairy tales about how to advance, in pain or silence, or both, across the landscape of male desire in order to claim some promised transformation. Now, since the dawn of the age of cinema, we can see the dreams and nightmares of our various cultures projected in paintings of light. We make gods, goddesses, and nymphs of the players, those debonair Apollos and gamine Daphnes, the mustache-twirling Jupiters, femme fatale Junos and relatable Ios, the modern Aphrodites whom we worship. And as with fairy tales, a number of our most affecting stories are still told through footwear.

Fairy tales themselves remain a fertile ground for inspiration, such as with the films of Disney, notably its 1950 animated *Cinderella* and the 2015 live-action remake. In the 1948 film *The Red Shoes*, the young female protagonist's desire to dance is extrapolated into a fable about adult female creative ambition and its ultimate destructiveness. Instead of village girl Karen, we get prima ballerina Vicky, whose romantic life is made impossible by her love for her work. Choosing one means losing all the rest, and the film ends tragically.

The list of iconic high heels and high heel references in film and television are seemingly endless. From the dancing Ferragamo platforms of Carmen Miranda in *Down Argentine Way* (1940) to Marilyn Monroe's white pumps perched over a subway grate in *The Seven Year Itch* (1955); to the thigh-high pleather boots of hooker Julia Roberts in *Pretty Woman* (1990), and the myriad icy stilettos of power player Robin Wright in *House of Cards* (2013). In *The Devil Wears Prada* (2006), sensibly shod Anne Hathaway refers to her glamorous female magazine colleagues as "the clackers," because of the sound made by their heels on the lobby floor. It's meant dismissively, the term bringing to mind the scuttering of grasping claws on a hard surface, scrambling for purchase, but by the end of the film, Hathaway's character is wearing them too, as part of her metamorphosis into sophistication. In *Some Like It Hot* (1959), Jack Lemmon's character chooses the name "Daphne" when he transforms himself into a high-heel-wearing woman, even though he and Tony Curtis's character had already decided that he'd be called "Geraldine." He then spends the rest of the film being pursued.

In the 1967 classic *Belle du Jour*, about a Parisian housewife turned prostitute named Séverine played by Catherine Deneuve, she spends most of the film in a pair of low, blocky-heeled "pilgrim pumps," which represent the bourgeois life she is trying to escape through her transgressions. By the final scene, she has changed at last into a pair of scallop-edged stilettos, as if to signal that she is conventional no more. Much of the plot, such as it is, revolves around her sexual fantasies, which are all about violence and degradation. But of course she herself is just a fantasy, the invention of the filmmaker, Luis Buñuel—a man fantasizing about the fantasies of a fantasy woman.

145

Perhaps the most famous pairs of shoes of the last century were themselves the stuff of cinema fairy tales, their function a *deus ex machina*. They are the ruby slippers from the 1939 film *The Wizard of Oz*, worn by a 16-year-old Judy Garland as Dorothy Gale. Now a part of the permanent collection of the National Museum of American History, the beloved costume heels are so popular among visitors that the carpet in front of the display case has had to be replaced multiple times due to heavy traffic.

Throughout most of the film, the shoes do nothing in the narrative except put Dorothy in danger—the Wicked Witch of the West wants the shoes, not the girl. It is almost a reversal of "Little Red Riding Hood," in that a piece of clothing given to her increases her danger, rather than defending her, as she ventures into the dark woods (although the red hood doesn't seem to contribute much, either). The ruby slippers neither protect Dorothy nor speed her way, and like Karen, she too cannot take off these red shoes. They are mute until the end, when suddenly, with three clicks of her heels, they fix everything.

In the L. Frank Baum fantasy novel on which the film was based, Dorothy is given silver slippers, like the Grimms' Cinderella on the first night of the ball. In an earlier silent film adaptation of the book, she isn't given any magical shoes at all. It was allegedly screenwriter Noel Langeley's idea to make the slippers made of rubies (or rather, red sequins), to best take advantage of the film's Technicolor production. The shoes are ultimately powerful in that they fuel Dorothy's adventure and solve her central problem in the end: how to get home to Kansas. But they also turn her into prey in a way that she wouldn't be without them.

Dorothy Gale may have escaped the fairy tale pain price that would normally accompany wearing shoes like the ruby slippers, but not so Judy Garland. She was put on a starvation diet by the film studio to which she was signed. During filming for *The Wizard of Oz*, the studio lot canteen was instructed to deny her all food except clear soups and cottage cheese. On top of that, her bosses fed her the 1930s equivalent of diet pills—speed. Unable to sleep due to the amphetamines, she was then given barbiturates to bring her down at night, and became addicted. After decades spent struggling with substance abuse, disordered eating, and depression, she died of an accidental overdose at age 47.

146

The vulnerability of a woman in high heels is part of the appeal, invoking affection and sympathy, at least for some. In the opening sequence of the 1953 film *Roman Holiday*— Audrey Hepburn's big debut—a young princess of an unnamed country (Hepburn) is seen on an exhausting state tour of Europe. After a long day, she must then stand to greet a seemingly endless line of dignitaries at a ball held in her honor. Her face is gracious, impassive, but the camera affords us a peak underneath the crinolines of her floor-length ball gown. There we see her tiredness expressed in the way that she lifts one foot out of her high heel to stretch her toes and relieve the pressure. It's a gesture that anyone who has worn high heels all day will instantly recognize. *She may be a princess, but really she's just like us*, it seems to say.

Later that night, fed up to the point of hysteria, she escapes the prison of her position and sneaks into the labyrinth of postwar Rome, where she meets not the Minotaur, but Gregory Peck. During her day spent enjoying the city, the first thing she does is ditch her high heels and buy a pair of flats. Then she cuts her hair short, eats gelato, and wanders through the ancient metropolis—*a part of a scene, anonymous, listening*, as Plath wanted to be—her two male chaperones allowing her to mingle with its inhabitants in ways that might not otherwise have gone as smoothly. It's a film about a young woman exhausted by obligations, who rebels for a day, but ultimately returns to her duties and the high heels that they require.

147

How can we retain and celebrate a woman's sexuality and femininity, while freeing her from sexual objecthood? What are women even like outside of patriarchy? As Virginia Woolf said, we don't actually know. Patriarchy is not a conventional prison, but rather a labyrinth, confusing even to its architects. The echoes are endless. According to Scottish artist Thomas Lawson, *Every cigarette, every drink, every love affair echoes down a never-ending passageway of references—to advertisements, to television shows, to movies—to the point where we no longer know if we mimic or are mimicked.* Sometimes a cigar is just a cigar, but can a woman's shoe ever be just a shoe? I trip in my high heels on some concrete steps near a row of cherry trees and fall, not just down the stairs, but down through cinema, and history, and fairy tales, and myth. I fall past CEOs and sex workers, past passionate suffragettes and doomed queens; past Ginger Rogers and Marie Antoinette, and Yexian, and Daphne with her toes sprouting laurel roots.

In a way, it is easier for a woman to consider rejecting high heels on political grounds if no one has ever questioned her right to them. High heels seem to do the most good when they allow an individual to come into contact with a persona or facet of themselves that either socially liberates them or touches on some deep aspect of identity they've been barred from reaching. If you've been told that you're too *something* to be allowed into the spaces of elegant or sexy femininity— too fat, too dark, to plain, to clumsy, too poor, too shy, too male—then wearing them can indeed be a powerful experience of transformation. Ignoring this does a great injustice. But it also doesn't erase high heels' other echoes that accompany even the most elevated forms of cultural femininity—objecthood, obligatory pain, sexual violence, and forced interiority. Both are true.

148

We are in a decades-long process of finding out what a free woman can look and act like, which will probably take centuries more to determine. We're still sorting out the relationship between glass ceilings and glass slippers. For now, the idea of doing something "in high heels" is a near-universally understood shorthand meaning both that the person doing it is female, and that in doing it, she faces additional, gendered challenges.

Two months before the 2016 American presidential election, when gendered politicking had reached a particular fever pitch, NPR producer Beth Novey penned a fed-up op-ed, asking *Can We Finally Stop Doing Things "Backwards And In*

Heels?" President Obama had recently introduced Secretary Hillary Clinton at the Democratic National Convention by saying that during their adversarial 2008 primary, *She was doing everything I was doing, but just like Ginger Rogers, it was backwards in heels.* The line comes from a 1982 Frank and Earnest cartoon in which a female character opines on a poster for Fred Astaire that, sure, he was great, but Rogers did everything he did, only backward and, well, you get it. Clinton herself used the phrase repeatedly throughout her two presidential campaigns and during her tenure as Secretary of State.

Novey pointed out that the phrase had been used at the DNC before, as early as 1988, by Texas treasurer Ann Richards, when she noted that, in 160 years, she was only the second woman to ever deliver the party's keynote address. Richards used the line as a sort of hardship brag for women's willingness to do twice the work for a fraction of the recognition and opportunity: "if you give us a chance, we can perform, backwards and in high heels!" The crowd applauded wildly.

Novey notes, *Ginger was doing everything backward because she lived in a world where only the Freds could go forward.* She posits some knowingly clunky alternatives to the stock phrase, like *concurrently, and with inadequate parental leave,* or *nervously, while trolled on social media,* before throwing up her writerly hands to say that in the meantime, at least a woman should be moving *forward— always forward—and in whatever shoes she wants.*

149

We write—or at least I do—in order to try and fit the storms that rage inside of us into a jar. We can never succeed, and much is lost. But still, in the end, something is preserved regardless. I've now spent so much time looking at and thinking about high heels that they've started to lose their familiarity to me. Like saying a word so many times in a row that its meaning and sounds warp, unmoor from unconscious association, and become alien, to the point that you ask yourself, really? Was it really like this the whole time? I haven't turned against high heels the way that one might expect, but they no longer seem quite so harmlessly normal.

I don't wear stilettos very often anymore, but that's mostly because my day job has changed—or at least, that is what I tell myself. The shoes I wear most days are a pair of ankle boots with a stacked leather heel of about two and a half inches. My partner calls these "high heels" but I don't really think of them that way. They're like seventeenth-century men's shoes, and for my purposes, they don't hurt. I spent too many years in stilettos to ever feel totally put together in a pair of flats. I am a creature of the environment that formed me.

150

Shoes are for feet, and feet are for walking, and when many walk together, it creates a path. When I tried to examine the path walked by women, I found it to be full of beasts and deception, setbacks and false starts. We are not yet out of our feminine glass labyrinth, and there's no telling how long it will take; at least it seems we have grasped a thread. How long will it be until we can end our fairy tale silence, and consider the pain price paid? Will things get worse for women before they get better? The answers lie around a bend we haven't reached yet. There's no telling how our ideas of masculinity and femininity will be transformed the closer we get to an exit. But as with all things—like the lost oceans described by Ovid in his *Metamorphoses*, where old ships' anchors are found on mountaintops, or the rivers that burst forth in the desert, aroused by ancient earthquakes—all we can know is that they will change.

ACKNOWLEDGMENTS

My thanks go first to the patient souls who made this book possible, in particular three men who never questioned the idea that feminism, Ovid, biology, and Borges could go together with high heels: editors Haaris Naqvi, Ian Bogost, and especially Christopher Schaberg, for his careful attention to the manuscript and that one out-of-the-blue, book-changing suggestion. I'd also like to thank everyone at Bloomsbury, as well as the Jean V. Naggar Literary Agency and my own agents there, Elizabeth Evans and Alice Tasman, for all their hard work behind the scenes.

The greatest of love and thanks to my dear friend Jasmine "Dee" Balgobin, whose unwavering affection and enthusiasm has meant everything to me throughout the writing of this book, and for the past twenty years; and to my family, Mom, Dad, Lea, Zack, June, Sienna, Aunt Melody, Dan, and Stefan. All my love and thanks also to my husband Michael L. Trujillo for his devotion and support.

Many people helped with the writing of this book through their friendship, scholarship, encouragement, or in other ways—in Paris, New York, and New Mexico—as well as through their own writing. I thank you all. Special thanks however go to Allison Devers for fortitude, and Rebecca Solnit for textual and political inspiration.

My brilliant friend Emily Rose Martinez died at age 25, but I once dreamed that I visited her in the city of death, where she lived in a beautiful apartment open to the sky, and had become a Che Guevara-style revolutionary hero. This one is for her.

SELECTED BIBLIOGRAPHY

Andersen, Hans Christian. *Hans Christian Andersen: Fairy Tales*. Translated by Tiina Nunnally. London: Penguin Classics, 2004.

Borges, Jorge Luis. *Labyrinths*. New York: New Directions, 1964.

Fairbairn, Daphne J. *Odd Couples: Extraordinary Differences between the Sexes in the Animal Kingdom*. Princeton: Princeton University Press, 2013.

Fisher, Eva Hagberg. "How I Learned to Look Believable." *New York Times*, January 3, 2018.

Friedan, Betty. *The Feminine Mystique*. New York: W.W. Norton & Company, 1963.

Grimm, Jacob and Wilhelm. *The Original Folk and Fairy Tales of the Brothers Grimm: The Complete First Edition*. Translated by Jack Zipes. Princeton: Princeton University Press, 2014.

Guéguen, Nicolas. "High Heels Increase Women's Attractiveness." *Archives of Sexual Behavior*, November 2014.

Hughes, Ted. *Collected Poems of Ted Hughes*. London: Faber and Faber, 2003.

Hughes, Ted. *Birthday Letters: Poems*. New York: Farrar, Straus and Giroux, 1998.

Hughes, Ted. *Phèdre: A Play*. Written by Jan Racine and translated by Ted Hughes. New York: Farrar, Straus and Giroux, 1998.

Karr, Mary. "Uninvent This: High Maintenance." *New Yorker*, May 16, 2016. https://www.newyorker.com/magazine/2016/05/16/down-with-high-heels

Koda, Harold. *100 Shoes: The Costume Institute / The Metropolitan Museum of Art*. Intr. Sarah Jessica Parker. New Haven: Yale University Press, 2001.

Krakauer, Jon. *Missoula: Rape and the Justice System in a College Town*. New York: Doubleday, 2015.

Molloy, John T. *The Woman's Dress for Success Book*. New York: Warner Books, 1977.

Morris, Paul H., et al. "High heels as supernormal stimuli: How wearing high heels affects judgements of female attractiveness." *Evolution & Human Behavior* 34, no. 3 (May 2013): 176–81.

Nicholson, Julia, and Anne-Laure Mercier. *In Their Shoes: Fairy Tales and Folktales*. London: Pushkin Press, 2016.

Novey, Beth. "Can We Finally Stop Doing Things 'Backwards And In Heels?'" *NPR* (August 4, 2016). https://www.npr.org/2016/08/04/488213995/can-we-finally-stop-doing-things-backwards-and-in-heels.

Ovid. *Metamorphoses.* Intr. Denis Feeney, tr. David Raeburn. London: Penguin Classics, 2016.

Perrault, Charles. *The Complete Fairy Tales of Charles Perrault*. Translated by Nicoletta Simborowski. Boston: Houghton Mifflin Harcourt, 1993.

Persson, Helen, et al. *Shoes: Pleasure and Pain*. London: V&A Publishing, 2015.

Plath, Sylvia. *The Bell Jar.* Portsmouth, UK: William Heinemann, 1963.

Plath, Sylvia. *Ariel.* London: Faber & Faber, 1965.

Plath, Sylvia. *The Unabridged Journals of Sylvia Plath*. New York: Anchor Books, 2000.

Plath, Sylvia. *Sylvia Plath: Drawings*. With Frieda Hughes. London: Faber & Faber, 2013.

Radnor, Abigail. "That's me in the picture: Ninalee Craig photographed by Ruth Orkin in Florence in 1951, aged 23." *Guardian*, January 30, 2015. https://www.theguardian.com/artanddesign/2015/jan/30/ninalee-craig-photograph-ruth-orkin-florence-1951

Scarry, Elaine. *The Body in Pain: The Making and Unmaking of the World.* New York: Oxford University Press, 1985.

Shawcross, Rebecca. *Shoes: An Illustrated History.* New York: Bloomsbury Visual Arts, 2014.

Small, Lisa, et al. *Killer Heels: The Art of the High-Heeled Shoe.* New York: Prestel USA, 2014.

Solnit, Rebecca. *Wanderlust: A History of Walking.* New York: Viking Press, 2000.

Solnit, Rebecca. *Men Explain Things To Me.* Chicago: Haymarket Books, 2015.

Solnit, Rebecca. "If I Were a Man." *Guardian*, August 26, 2017. https://www.theguardian.com/lifeandstyle/2017/aug/26/rebecca-solnit-if-i-were-a-man

Steele, Valerie, and Colleen Hill. *Shoe Obsession.* New Haven: Yale University Press, 2013.

Taga, Carlee. *Maybe She's Born with It: Analyzing Theories of Beauty from Biology, Society and the Media.* Thesis, Regis University. May 2012.

Tolentino, Jia. "How 'Empowerment' Became Something for Women to Buy." *New York Times*, April 12, 2016.

Tolentino, Jia. "The Case Against Contemporary Feminism." *New Yorker*, February 8, 2017. https://www.newyorker.com/books/page-turner/the-case-against-contemporary-feminism.

Tolentino, Jia. "Beauty and the Bestiality." *New Yorker*, March 27, 2017. https://www.newyorker.com/culture/jia-tolentino/beauty-and-the-bestiality.

Valenti, Jessica. *The Purity Myth: How America's Obsession with Virginity Is Hurting Young Women.* Berkeley: Seal Press, 2009.

Valenti, Jessica. "SlutWalks and the future of feminism." *Washington Post*, June 3, 2011. https://www.washingtonpost.com/opinions/slutwalks-and-the-future-of-feminism/2011/06/01/AGjB9LIH_story.html?noredirect=on&utm_term=.19f5ba7f8ea3.

Wolf, Naomi. *The Beauty Myth: How Images of Beauty Are Used Against Women*. London: Chatto & Windus, 1990; New York: Harper Perennial, 2002.

Woolf, Virginia. *The Death of the Moth and Other Essays*. New York: Harcourt Brace & Company, 1942.

Woolf, Virginia. *On Being Ill*. London: Hogarth Press, 1930.

INDEX